D0935298

British Farming in the
Great Depression

STUDIES IN HISTORICAL GEOGRAPHY

General Editors   Alan R. H. Baker *University Lecturer in Geography and Fellow of Emmanuel College, Cambridge* and J. B. Harley *Montefiore Reader in Geography at the University of Exeter*

PUBLISHED

Alan R. H. Baker   *Geographical Interpretations of Historical Sources:*
   John D. Hamshere and   *Readings in Historical Geography (1970)*
   John Langton (eds)   *Geography (1970)*
Josiah Cox Russell   *Medieval Regions and Their Cities (1972)*
Alan R. H. Baker (ed)   *Progress in Historical Geography(1972)*
Alan R. H. Baker and   *Man Made the Land: Essays in English Historical*
   J. B. Harley (eds)   *Geography (1973)*
P. J. Perry   *British Farming in the Great Depression 1870–1914: An Historical Geography (1974)*

IN PREPARATION

Australia: an Historical Geography   Michael Williams

Celts, Saxons and Vikings: Studies in Settlement Continuity   Glanville R. J. Jones

English Market Towns before the Industrial Revolution   J. H. C. Patten

English Provincial Cities of the Nineteenth Century   David Ward

Finland, Daughter of the Sea   Michael R. H. Jones

Historical Geography: an Introduction   Alan R. H. Baker

Historical Geography of Rural Settlement in Britain   Brian K. Roberts

A Social Geography of Britain in the Nineteenth Century   D. R. Mills

South America: an Historical Geography   D. J. Robinson

History through Maps   J. B. Harley

Tithe Surveys   Hugh C. Prince and Roger J. P. Kain

British Farming in the Great Depression 1870-1914

An Historical Geography

P. J. Perry

Senior Lecturer in Geography
University of Canterbury
Christchurch, NZ

David & Charles : Newton Abbot

For my Parents

0 7153 6267 4

Set in Times New Roman
and printed in Great Britain
by Bristol Typesetting Company Limited
for David & Charles (Holdings) Limited
South Devon House Newton Abbot Devon

Contents

Illustrations

FIGURES

DRAWINGS

Preface

'GOOD WINE NEEDS no bush' and historical geography should require no methodological apologia. As scholarship it must be judged on its substantive historical and geographical merits, as a contribution to, an extension and deepening of, our knowledge of the world. Is it true? Does it make sense? Nevertheless an historical geography without a methodological preface has come to be a rarity, and many such prefaces claim to introduce a novel, and implicitly a better, approach, be it retrospective or regressive, cross-sectional or chronological. At best, and not infrequently, the approach is refreshingly new, adding to insight and understanding; but on other occasions it entails a narrowing of focus, a blurring of vision, an impoverishment of understanding.

No such methodological claim is advanced in this avowedly and determinedly pragmatic study. It is tailored on the one hand to the topic, on the other to the available sources. The sector by sector approach pursued in the greater part of the book is, I am sure, an appropriate method for only a few historical geographies; indeed it does not suffice for the whole of this study.

The book was conceived as necessarily a mixture of history and geography, spiced with agriculture and economics, brought together to illuminate a phenomenon and problem. Should this be regarded as a definition of historical geography rather than a statement of working principles, it will at least serve to focus attention on the need to match method to materials and problems, to select an approach which aims to maximise understanding. Not all geographical writing appears in this light in the 1970s. The message matters more than the medium. As methodology is pragmatic so are conclusions interim; they are my findings, my understandings in 1972, not the last word or last judgement. I am sure that such an emphasis is particularly needful for historical geographers, who, I suspect, are more than averagely tempted by a wealth of tasks to be done to regard that which has been carried out as complete.

I have tried then to explain what happened to British farming in the last quarter of the nineteenth century, and only incidentally and secondarily to demonstrate an appropriate methodology for this end. The less evident and obtrusive this latter, the more pleased will I be. Like the farmer heroes of this book—if historical geography be allowed heroes—I prefer pragmatic profit and pleasure to doctrinaire and dogmatic decay.

In writing this book I have been helped by very many people in very many ways. Written in the University of Canterbury, Christchurch, NZ, it owes a great deal to my colleagues in the geography department—academic, technical and secretarial—to my students, to numerous visitors, and to friends throughout the university. I must, therefore, gladly acknowledge my considerable debt to my teachers and supervisors, Geoffrey Hewitt, Clifford Smith, and Jean Mitchell. A generous grant from the Erskine Fund of the University of Canterbury made possible a working visit to British libraries and universities to use material not readily available in New Zealand.

Without libraries and record offices, books about the past would be impossible to write. The invariable and unfailing helpfulness, forbearance, and courtesy of their staff is acknowledged, in particular the following: University of Canterbury, Canterbury Public Library (Christchurch, NZ), Lincoln College (Christchurch, NZ), General Assembly (Wellington, NZ), University of Cambridge, British Museum, Dorset County Museum, Dorset County Record Office, Bedfordshire County Record Office, and Digby Estate Office (Sherborne).

I also wish to thank a number of individuals who have been

particularly helpful: Dr R. G. Cant, Dr R. J. Johnston, Professor W. B. Johnston, Dr A. H. Grey, J. A. Frampton, Professor J. T. Coppock, the late T. W. Fletcher, Professor M. J. Wise, J. J. MacGregor, Mrs Judy Robertson, Miss Noelene Frew, G. W. Armitage, I. R. Perry, and Miss Gillian Samways. My greatest debt of all I acknowledge in the dedication.

P. J. PERRY

Christchurch and Sherborne

1
The Context of the Depression

THE STUDY OF agricultural change has by no means suffered from scholarly neglect during the last half-century; more particularly the last decade or so has seen a substantial reshaping of the hitherto accepted view of the course and pattern of events during the last three or four centuries—the Agricultural Revolution as it is commonly and loosely termed. A longer span of time, a wider territorial and technical base, have replaced an older focus on the 'new' rotations of eighteenth-century East Anglia and its squires.[1] The fact remains that while some aspects and periods have received considerable attention—such phases of growth and prosperity as the 1850s and 1860s,[2] for example—others have been neglected. Decay and dereliction are topics which appeal to relatively few scholars, agricultural historians and geographers among them; a Richard Jefferies may find there pathos or even a wry humour,[3] but most academics prefer the seemingly more important and potentially more heroic topics of growth, innovation and revolution.

The depression, whether or not the term is an accurate description, which afflicted rural Britain during the last quarter of the nineteenth century and which finally and completely disappeared only in the 1940s is academically ill-favoured in several respects. The period just beyond living memory is a notoriously difficult one for the scholar; objective truth and uncertain hearsay recollection are confused and intertwined; documentary material is abundant, but it is uneven in quality, and access is sometimes restricted. Nor is the late nineteenth

13

century so recent a period as to benefit—or perhaps to suffer —from the insatiable present-day appetite for instant and contemporary history. Moreover the phenomenon in question is the transference of agriculture, farming and the landed interest, from a position in the forefront of British polity, economy, and society to a relatively minor role. Agriculture accounted for 20 per cent of the gross national product in the late 1850s but for only 6 per cent in the late 1890s;[4] it employed over one-fifth of the population in 1851 but less than one-tenth in 1901. The topic contains within itself the seeds of its neglect by scholars.

Another feature of the depression has influenced the character of this book. Whether or not the term depression be an adequate description, it remains true that its causes are generally better understood and better known than its characteristics or its consequences. This is not to imply that those caught up in the depression were quite clear and quite correct in their understanding of events. Cause, characteristic, and consequence are not easily disentangled, and it is no simple matter for the scholar to determine where analysis and narrative should begin. However, there remains little doubt that falling prices, whatever their fundamental mechanism, and adverse seasons, wrought major, and for the participants uncomfortable, changes in British agriculture and rural society from the 1870s until World War I. The records of the time serve as a reminder that what happened was more than simple destruction and dereliction. The term depression is too well established to be given up, but it is arguable that discussion should focus as much or more upon the antecedents and development of new farming methods which were eventually to enjoy prosperity and stability—a whole range of grassland systems, for example—than upon spectacular but transient catastrophe and disaster.

THE LATE VICTORIAN SETTING

Late Victorian Britain was a rich and prosperous society, increasingly and unprecedentedly so; but wealth and power remained concentrated in the hands of the few, even though they were beginning to be shared with the many. The farm worker received the vote, a secret vote, in 1884; he remained one of the worst paid workers, but there is ample evidence that despite the disappearance of agricultural prosperity he was able to maintain his recently elevated standard of living at a level which might sometimes be described as comfortable. The point must not be exaggerated—there was no old age pension, no national health service—but by comparison with conditions earlier in the century this great leap forward represents a very significant change.

From 1851, however, Britain was more an urban and manufacturing nation than a rural and agricultural society; at the end of the century only 23 per cent of the population were rural, and less than 9 per cent gained their living in agriculture.[5] Growing towns, and an emptying, perhaps a moribund, countryside were characteristic features of the period. It was industry, and in particular industrial exports, which formed the base of Britain's wealth and power; but this wealth and power itself was less surely pre-eminent than it had been in mid-century. Not only were some basic industries, such as iron and steel, experiencing difficulties which have led some scholars to apply the epithet depression to the 1880s and 1890s, but foreign competitors, Germany and the USA in particular, were proving increasingly tough economic rivals. However, Britain's political, and especially naval, power remained so certain and considerable as to allow a growing dependence on imported food to be taken almost for granted; it was a necessity if the urban and industrial population was to be adequately and cheaply fed. Britain's economic and political power was thus an essential underpinning of agriculture's misfortunes. That the nation would and could be fed safely from overseas was a new, perhaps revolutionary, concept. Its almost unconscious acceptance reflected not only Britain's strength but also the success of European, very often British, colonisation in the New World. The decision to cut the British farmer's throat was taken in Westminster; the operation was carried out by his Canadian cousin, his New Zealand nephew, and by those more than usually ambitious and energetic of his labourers who, discontented with prospects at home, chose the American or Australian wheat frontier. Less wealthy and less self-assured, though more egalitarian, peasant societies in continental Europe were less prepared to proceed upon the same lines, probably less well equipped to do so; hence there exists, a century later, the highly protectionist agricultural policy of the European Common Market, its problem of agricultural overpopulation, and the great disparity between agricultural prices inside and outside its external tariff wall.[6]

Agriculture then appears to have enjoyed a diminishing role and importance in the economy and society of late Victorian Britain. The country landowner, however, remained an important figure in national politics, and farmer and landowner were usually pre-eminent in rural affairs. The fact that very many landowners had industrial as well as agricultural sources of income protected, though imperfectly, their national political status and often benefited their tenants' purses during the depression.[7] At the more local level, however, their position, although substantially protected by the relative inaccessibility of rural Britain, undoubtedly weakened during this period. This isolation was only partly overcome by the latter stage of filling out the railway network with secondary and branch lines in the last quarter of the century. The bicycle also had some effect, in particular among the working classes.[8] Nevertheless a generation which takes ready access to the countryside by means of a motor vehicle for granted requires to make a powerful imaginative leap to comprehend the remoteness of much of late nineteenth-century rural Britain, and the ease with which it could be forgotten or ignored by the majority of the population. The country house party was an important late nineteenth-century institution for the ruling class, but penetration, let alone understanding, by the middle and even working class—the Londoners' weekend in the country, for example—are developments of the inter-war years. Rural Britain was then in most respects a *terra incognita* to the masses—witness the many stories of slum Sunday school outings. It could be ignored by the urban middle class, and sacrificed by the political élite.

The countryside was changing in other respects than the agricultural, however. Compulsory education, near universal literacy, which it had long been possible to take for granted in Scotland, was attained in Britain as a whole in the last decades of the century. Literacy enhanced the selective character of rural depopulation, strengthened the position of the rural agitator, and in many cases exacerbated already uncertain personal relationships between master and man. The country newspaper, as often Liberal as Conservative, enjoyed a heyday of prosperity and bulk; and by the end of the century the bicycle, a shorter working week, a higher standard of living, gave at least the young farm worker a high degree of everyday mobility. Trade unions, however, enjoyed only ephemeral success among the farm workers, notably in the 1870s, in an area which they have always found difficult; but it may be argued that their no more than ephemeral strength played an important part in enabling farm workers to maintain money wages, and to increase real wages, during the depression.[9] No doubt rural Britain remained a strongly hierarchical society, at best benevolently paternalistic, at worst repressively authoritarian, but it was diminishingly so. The agricultural labourer could vote, elected county councils replacing the oligarchic quarter sessions in 1888. The massive turnover of tenant farmers and the legal protection of their rights and interests from 1875 onwards further weakened the landlord's position.[10] while in some areas the provision of smallholdings facilitated the labourer's economic and social progress.[11] Many country livings became pluralities, fewer parsons were scions of the local gentry, and many fewer took their place on the bench as justices of the peace. The depression itself forced upon many landowners reduced social and political activity, and in some cases the final humiliation of non-residence.

The countryside could easily be forgotten, by politician and proletariat alike, in late nineteenth-century Britain; Irish home rule, the navy, India, the increasing power of international competitors, were evidently more interesting and more important topics. Yet the seeds of rural social as well as economic change were sown, legislatively and technologically, falteringly and at time inadvertently; in most cases they were to come to fruition in later generations, if at all. By comparison agricultural depression in the stricter sense had an instantaneous effect as important as its long-term consequences.

B

BRITISH FARMING IN THE NINETEENTH CENTURY

During the nineteenth century farmers and landowners experienced, in succession, prosperity and adversity, a course of events not always as expected, and which did not always engender a rational reaction. No doubt the total and the individual experience, reality and myth, were important determinants of the way both groups responded to late nineteenth-century circumstances. Farmers are almost as notoriously inclined to reminisce as they are to grumble, and, while by the 1880s very few could personally recall the agricultural prosperity during the Napoleonic wars, many were only too ready to recall postwar depression, the events of 1846, and the golden age of the 1850s and 1860s, with enthusiasm if not always with accuracy.

Early in the century war with France had pushed the price of wheat to unprecedentedly high levels—in 1812 the official figure reached 126s 6d (£6.32) a quarter, bringing high profits to the farmer, rising rents to the landlord, and at times near starvation to the labourer. The war economy, however transient, also favoured investment and improvement, most notably the last great wave of enclosure, of marginal land in particular, some of it dubiously profitable in the long run. Wheat paid the farmer very well, and the British farmers' traditional faith and delight in corn growing, at worst an obsession, was strengthened by this experience, even though its origins are much more ancient.

The postwar agricultural depression was predictable and severe, but overshadowed on the one hand by widespread political and social unrest and on the other by the desperate position of the farm labourer, epitomised by events at Tolpuddle in 1834. However, the 1830s and 1840s witnessed the return of some agricultural prosperity, and in particular the advent of important innovations in the theory and practice of farming—the establishment of the Royal Agricultural Society and its college at Cirencester in 1838 and 1845 respectively, and the perfection and consequential cheapening of tile drainage, for example.[12] But the great obsession of the period was first the prospect and then, more briefly, the results of Corn Law repeal. Most farmers and many landlords were its strenuous adversaries. Repeal did produce a short-lived and severe depression, often recalled later in the century, but the agricultural prosperity of the 1850s and 1860s soon made the Corn Laws and protection a very dead issue.

The basis of this most prosperous period was a system of high investment for high returns, justified by high prices: between 1850 and 1875 the price of wheat fell below 40s (£2) a quarter only in 1851, reaching 74s (£3.70) in 1855 and 64s (£3.20) in 1867.[13] Wages, which averaged, inasmuch as the concept is meaningful, about 9s (45p) a week in the early 1850s had reached 13s (65p) by the early 1870s.[14] Likewise rents, about 20s (£1) an acre in the early 1850s, reached a peak of almost 30s (£1.50) in the mid-1870s.[15] The heart of the system was investment by landlord and farmer alike— long-term in buildings, medium-term in drainage and pedigree livestock, short-term in feeds and fertilisers. It was this agri-culture which collapsed and had to be replaced in the last decades of the century. Cereal cultivation in association with livestock production was its most conspicuous feature: 'The plough was kept going to the same extent as under the Corn Laws, the numbers of livestock increased, and the value of agricultural land also increased'.[16] By repute the plough was the moneymaker, although dependent in this respect on the manure produced by the livestock. In fact such a view was probably increasingly inaccurate; livestock was the paying proposition but no adequate system of cost accounting existed to make this plain.[17]

It is, however, misleading to speak and think of a single system of high farming basic to the prosperity of the mid-century. Rather the pattern outlined above was the apex of an agricultural pyramid made up of a diversity of systems varying in form, efficiency and profitability. The pattern was, nevertheless, aspired to by a large number of farmers, and was the object of numerous retrospective glances and com-ments when hard times came. Money was not hard to come by in farming at this period: 'They did not have to make money, it was brought home and shot down at their doors' was one farmer's subsequent comment.[18] It was commonplace later in the century to comment that 20 years of prosperity

had made farmers 'soft' and given them expectations of an
unduly high standard of living.[19] Moreover they had come to
take for granted the adequacy of the system they were following; changes taking place were more 'a general upheaval of
the middling and the worst' towards the standards of the
best than a radical reorientation.[20] Prosperity, however, resulted not from any permanent advantage or technical perfection enjoyed by the British, but from wars in Russia and
the USA, traditional and potential competitors, and from the
imperfect technology of the early railways and the first generation of steamers. Had the ephemeral character of these advantages been appreciated, a more cautious attitude to long- and
medium-term investment might have prevailed. That such
caution was rare suggests some lack of foresight; but the temptation to believe that good times will never end, complacently
to accept the profitable status quo, has ever been almost
irresistible.

Throughout the century Britain was for the most part an
agrarian society of landlords and tenants, and no longer, if
it ever had been, a society of peasant proprietors or owner-
occupiers (save locally and as a minority).[21] Landlord and
tenant were usually on good terms, more often because most
landlords were resident for at least part of the year, hunting
and shooting, occupying pew and bench, alongside their
tenants, than because the tenants were protected by covenants, leases, agreements, or the law. The system depended on
trust, goodwill, and personal contact; it broke down most often
where, as in Wales, for example, politics, religion and non-
residence destroyed these qualities.[22] Most landlords, and
their agents, chose tenants for vacant farms with great care,
commonly preferring local applicants and members of tenant
families. Only rarely was public advertisement required.[23]
More often the agent was deluged with applications.[24] The
integrity of the estate was usually, though not completely, protected by the family settlement, in preparing which the family
solicitor was the key figure. Exceptions to all these circumstances existed, commonly of a regional character, such as
those engendered by the distinctive Scottish legal system;
but for the most part, in prosperous periods in particular,
there was little reason to doubt the stability, the settled

character, of the landlord and tenant facet of rural society.

The experience of depression varied as much through space as through time. Not all areas, not all farming systems, and certainly not all individuals suffered equally or simultaneously. In general the cereal producer has been regarded as the chief victim, simply because he complained loudest and longest, and his prices demonstrably fell furthest; the livestock producer, the dairyman in particular, appears to have suffered less. The physical environment, and to some extent the cultural, were also of some importance, the heavy clays and the poorer upland soils providing the most difficult technical environment, and the way of life common in the highland zone adding distinctive features to that area's experience of depression. Proximity (and access) to urban markets was a third significant geographical factor.

Arable-livestock systems, the epitome of the high farming of the 1850s and 1860s, were practised widely throughout the lowland zone: East Anglia, Northumberland and the Lothians, much of the chalk and limestone escarpment country—though certainly not all of it—were areas widely following this pattern. The Shorthorn and Lincoln Red, and such sheep breeds as the Suffolk and Oxford Down, were its essential livestock.[25] Drainage, artificial fertilisers, and solid buildings—some of them embarrassingly so to farmers a century later—were other essentials, though often unprofitable in the long run to the landlords who provided them. Less fertile areas, the heaviest clays in particular, were farmed less intensively, often still on almost medieval lines—a triennial rotation of wheat, beans and fallow with some livestock. This system, and the soils which necessitated it, had long been condemned, but it paid in good seasons, required little capital, and was believed to be the only practicable system by many of its practitioners. Not surprisingly such farmers often failed early in the depression, in Essex and Bedfordshire, for example. Their problem was compounded by the reputed—sometimes real—difficulty of laying down good pasture in these areas until almost the end of the century. As a Suffolk proverb put it: 'To break a pasture will make a man; to make a pasture will break a man'.[26] At the other end of the spectrum were poor thin upland soils, broken up during prosperous times from pasture to arable, which suffered during the depression from diminished inputs of artificial fertiliser and manure. Many contemporaries noted the retreat of cereal cultivation from such hills,[27] which were among the last localities to recover from the depression. The Cotswolds were an example.

Three other agricultural systems were important in the lowland zone—grazing, dairying, and market gardening. All tended to expand at the expense of intensive arable-livestock farming during the depression.

Grazing took a number of forms. The best known was the fattening of cattle on the finest and oldest Midland pastures, notably in Leicestershire and Northamptonshire. Romney Marsh and West Dorset concentrated on grassland sheep, the latter, in producing out of season Dorset Horn lambs for the Christmas market, exemplifying the specialised as well as localised character of much grazing. The grazing of cattle in particular was thought of as the rich man's domain: 'If a man can live by grazing he can live without it'.[28] This was a question not only of the capital investment and risks involved, but also no doubt of the appeal of a system demanding limited day to day attention and considerable technical and commercial judgement, while offering the prospect of residence in good hunting country. Shrewdness in buying and selling was the grazier's stock in trade; most people assumed late in the nineteenth century that grass, his crop, could be taken for granted.

Dairying was, by comparison, the least esteemed and fashionable branch of farming, not so much because little capital was needed as because constant attention, particularly milking, was required, and a large part of this labour input commonly had to come from the farmer and his family. Even before the prosperity of the 1850s and 1860s this task had no appeal for farmers' wives and daughters with increasingly fashionable and middle-class pretensions.[29] Until the depression was well advanced, fresh milk production was less important than butter and cheese making to the dairy farmer.

However, as the urban population increased and prospered, as disease and health regulations forced the closure of urban dairies, as cheese and butter imports increased and the railways system filled out, this situation was reversed.[30] The traditional strongholds of dairying such as Ayrshire, Cheshire, and Somerset shared this process with new developments around the main towns, near the railways (around Swindon in the late 1870s, for example),[31] and in districts that had once been arable (much of Essex, for example).[32] The town-supplying dairy farmer feared no overseas competition, and his rent and his feeding-stuff bill fell during the depression; but labour remained a problem even with the abandonment of cheese and butter making, and the cost and conditions of carrying milk to market were a second area where difficulties sometimes arose.[33]

Horticulture and fruit growing rivalled dairying as farming's growth sector during the depression. They were less the beneficiaries of natural protection than dairying: for example, many Channel Island horticultural enterprises developed for a British market during the depression years.[34] Demand was excellent, particularly in terms of potential for expansion. Like the dairyman the market gardener turned over his capital quickly, during this period a considerable advantage over the cereal or livestock producer.[35] In some instances very little initial capital was needed, some branches of horticulture providing an ideal entry to farming for the small man. So much was this the case that horticulture was not generally thought of as farming.[36] However, land which did not pay under traditional arable systems was cheaply turned over to horti‑culture in some districts during the depression—in the Fens and the West Riding, for example.[37] More capital-intensive types of enterprise, like tree-fruit cultivation, also expanded, benefiting from an established system of agreement with landowners for the protection of tenant investment.[38] Thus the orchard acreage increased by over 60 per cent between 1873 and 1904.[39] A parallel development was specialised poultry farming, around Heathfield in Sussex, for example.[40]

Some districts in the highland zone were as famous for arable-livestock husbandry, for grazing, for dairying, and for horticulture as the lowland zone. Perthshire and Lanark were renowned for soft fruit, as was South Wales for dairying. But pre-eminently the north and west were the domain of the livestock breeder, the seller of store stock to the lowland feeder and fattener. Some localities and many individuals fed as well as bred, and most grew some cereals and other crops as supplementary feed to carry stock through the winter. Store stock remained the mainstay of the economy, the breeder depending on what the feeder felt his market allowed him to pay. The feeder was thus at one end of the line, by the last quarter of the century usually a railway. He was no middle-man readily able to adjust prices and costs to provide a margin. On the other hand his capital investment was relat-ively small; he needed to make relatively few cash payments, his stock, his feeding stuffs, and even his labour force being primarily home-bred. He had few illusions as to his position. In hard times the breeder's characteristic response was to increase stock if possible, and to accept a lower—sometimes appallingly low—standard of living. These possibilities made the livestock rearer rather less prone to failure, less likely to be forced out of farming in these circumstances, than the cereal producer. Characteristically family farms employing relatively little hired labour were common in these areas. Even when times were hard, keen competition for farms prevented rents from falling far in these districts.[41] Emigra-tion was commonplace: to cite a New Zealand example, the Taranaki 'cow cocky' is often of Devon or Cornwall ancestry.[42] Experience with livestock, a capacity for hard work, willing-ness to accept a lower standard of living than most lowlanders expected, made the migrant Scot or Welshman almost the typical new tenant of a rundown low-rented farm in south-eastern England.[43]

During the depression the general tendency was for the area of arable-livestock high farming to contract at the expense of grassland farming or horticulture. Thus in Oxfordshire the wheat acreage fell by 45 per cent between 1874 and 1900, and the area of permanent pasture increased by 41 per cent. Correspondingly cattle numbers increased—from 4·7 million in the early 1870s to 5·8 million in 1906–10—and their average age fell sharply. Sheep numbers fell, mainly because of the decline of arable-livestock farming in the lowland zone—

Oxfordshire had almost 350,000 sheep and lambs in 1874 and only 232,000 in 1900—but there was no comparable decline in the highland zone.[44] There the acceptance of a lower standard of living, the abandonment of marginal land, and migration were the hallmarks of a less conspicuous but not necessarily less keenly felt depression. On an objective view the former area of depressed rentals, farms to let, and an unkempt countryside was no doubt the more depressed, but it is to be questioned whether a strictly objective view is adequate.

The several most characteristic features of the depression embrace a wide degree of geographical variation. The total impact of the depression was catastrophic in parts of Essex and Huntingdonshire, but slight in Lancashire and Cheshire. The price of wheat fell throughout Britain, as did the rural population, though the latter fall was uneven and imperfectly related to the incidence of depression. Changes in cereal acreage were a response to lower prices, but spatially they were far from uniform; likewise rents, which fell by generally less than 10 per cent—in some cases not at all—in the highland zone, fell by as much as 50 per cent in parts of the lowland zone.[45] Adverse seasons were widely discussed, but were not uniformly disastrous.

The favoured geographical parameters of the depression have been those of land use—declining cereal acreages and the increasing importance of permanent grass. The historical parameters were prices and rents. These visible and measurable changes recorded in contemporary statistics are readily mapped and easily understood. Some geographical features relevant if not central to the depression tended to disappear during this period—the long-standing and significant differences between farm labourers' wages and productivity in the north and the south, for instance, and the lack of uniformity in the agricultural labour market.[46] On the other hand there is verbal and statistical evidence suggesting that during the depression local or personal advantages—better soil, more skilful and enterprising marketing—all extremely difficult to measure, became more rather than less important, and that the geographical diversity of the agricultural situation increased rather than diminished.

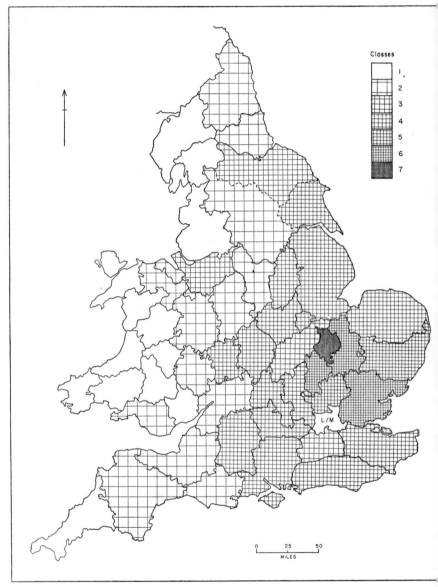

Fig 1 Agricultural failure (assignments and bankruptcies, annual average by counties), 1881–3, as a percentage of the farming population in 1881: (1) less than 0·1 per cent; (2) 0·1 per cent to less than 0·2 per cent; (3) 0·2 per cent to less than 0·3 per cent; (4) 0·3 per cent to less than 0·4 per cent; (5) 0·4 per cent to less than 0·5 per cent; (6) 0·5 per cent to less than 0·6 per cent; (7) more than 0·6 per cent. L/M, London and Middlesex

Are there, however, any characteristics of the depression which provide an overview or summation, temporal and spatial, of the experience of depression? One class of material whose usefulness in this context has been demonstrated relates to bankruptcy;[47] no doubt comparably useful material awaits exploitation elsewhere. The very term depression indicates the commercial and business problems faced by farmers, culminating in the complete failure, the bankruptcy, of an unfortunate few. Such complete failure was always exceptional—at worst perhaps one in twenty or thirty farmers failed in the most severely affected parts of Huntingdonshire in the crisis of the early 1880s—but there is no reason to believe that this extreme was not spatially correlated with the broader incidence of depression.

Maps of farmer bankruptcies for the period 1881-3, the latter part of the first acutely depressed period, indicate that the depression was more severe in the lowland than the highland zone (Fig 1). In all but two counties south and east of a line from Hampshire to the East Riding more than 0·3 per cent of all farmers failed each year, but in most of Wales and the North West less than 0·1 per cent. The more localised patterns are also apparent, in the misfortunes of heavy land localities, in Essex and along the Lower Trent, for example. For the period 1891-3, part of a second very hard period, a broadly similar pattern emerges, except that signs of recovery appear in formerly very depressed areas extending northwards from London to the Wash (Fig 2). Changes in the law of bankruptcy invalidate absolute comparison of the two periods, however. It is also interesting to note that this same spatial pattern, although not its absolute dimensions, appears for the period 1871-3, part of the Indian summer of prosperous high farming (Fig 3). The spatial pattern of failure and difficulty which appears during the depression is not necessarily a new one, it may merely make manifest a long-standing geography of farming risks. However, whereas in the latter three-year period there were about twenty times as many farmer bankruptcies in the most severely as in the least severely affected counties (*pro rata* with the number of farmers) for the early 1870s the comparable ratio is only ten to one, evidence of an accentuation of an established spatial pattern, and perhaps of the in-

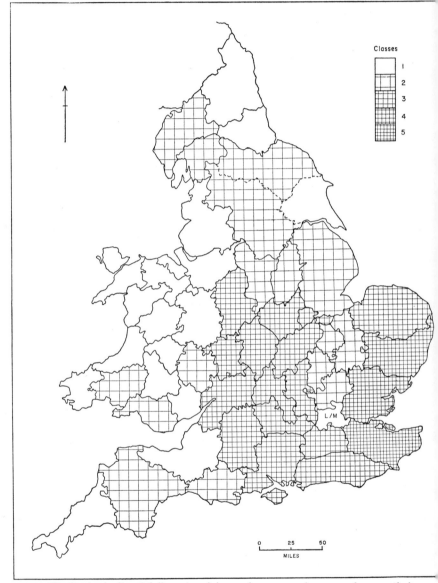

Fig 2 Agricultural failure (receiving orders—annual average by counties),
1891–3, as a percentage of the farming population in 1891: (1) less than
0·05 per cent; (2) 0·05 per cent to less than 0·10 per cent; (3) 0·10 per cent
to less than 0·15 per cent; (4) 0·15 per cent to less than 0·20 per cent; (5)
more than 0·20 per cent. L/M, London and Middlesex

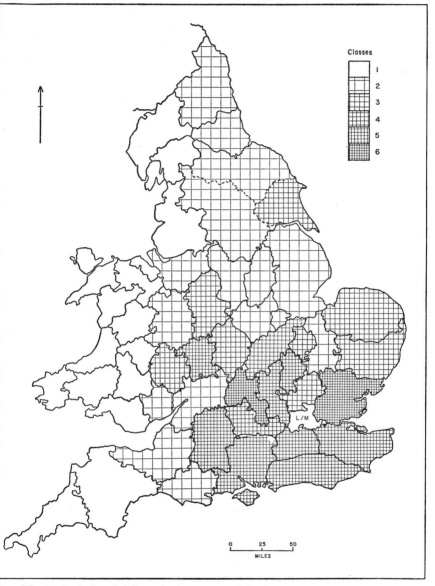

Fig 3 Agricultural failure (assignments and bankruptcies, annual average by counties), 1871–3, as a percentage of the farming population in 1871: (1) less than 0·04 per cent; (2) 0·04 per cent to less than 0·08 per cent; (3) 0·08 per cent to less than 0·12 per cent; (4) 0·12 per cent to less than 0·16 per cent; (5) 0·16 per cent to less than 0·20 per cent; (6) more than 0·20 per cent. L/M, London and Middlesex

creased importance of local advantages or disadvantages of
soil and situation and of the individual's response to them.

As has been noted, the depression was a dynamic rather
than a static phenomenon; it is doubtful whether a broad and
instantaneous geography of the depression derived from bankruptcies, rents, acreages, or 'farm sales' can give a realistic
view of it, except as it was seen by minority groups such as
Royal Commissions and their itinerant assistants, farming
journalists and politicians, who alone were able to obtain such
a perspective. Many landowners, probably most farmers, were
in no position and no mood to adopt this viewpoint; their complaint of depression related present to past experience, and it
was to be heard even in objectively well favoured counties such
as Cumberland and Westmorland. Is it possible to recon-
struct a geography of this subjective view of the depression?
Comparison of bankruptcy data for 1881–3 with that for
1871–3 (Fig 4) goes some way in this direction: the counties
around the Wash and parts of the East Midlands became the
depression heartland, but the map also draws attention to some
western counties; variation in the incidence of depression
from most to least affected county is reduced from about
twenty times on a static view to about six times. Comparison
of the early 1890s with the early 1880s (Fig 5) suggests that
by this date the depression was as keenly felt in many northern
and western as in southern and eastern counties; absence of
distress in earlier years makes the later depression seem the
more severe, although a number of anomalies, and questions,
are raised, such as the more favourable experience of north-
west than south-west Wales. Comparison of the early 1890s
with the early 1870s is of more dubious validity (Fig 6). How
many farmers had survived twenty bad years? It does suggest
a contrast between the position of dairying and arable farming
on the one hand and rearing on the other in both a subjective
and objective view of the depression.

The importance of perception of the depression as well as
its reality has been emphasised at several points. There is no
doubt that extreme misperception was at times important, in
the persistent, perhaps wilful, exaggeration of the role of the
weather in early years and the resultant inhibition of desirable
changes. The work of Olson and Harris places the arable

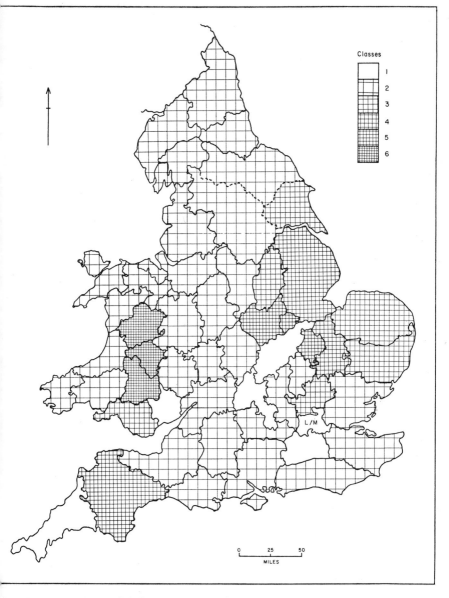

Fig 4 Agricultural failures, 1881–3 (a) in relation to agricultural failures, 1871–3 (b), (a/b): (1) less than 1·5; (2) 1·5 to less than 3·0; (3) 3·0 to less than 4·5; (4) 4·5 to less than 6·0; (5) 6·0 to less than 7·5; (6) more than 7·5. L/M, London and Middlesex

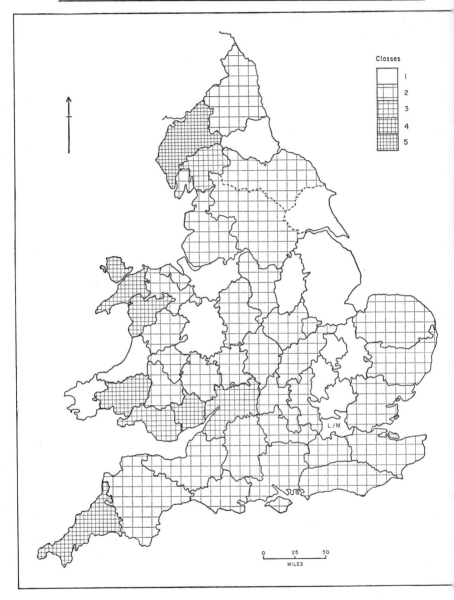

Fig 5   Agricultural failures, 1891–3 (a) in relation to agricultural failures, 1881–3 (b), (a/b): (1) less than 0·33; (2) 0·33 to less than 0·67; (3) 0·67 to less than 1·0; (4) 1·0 to less than 1·33; (5) more than 1·33. L/M, London and Middlesex

farmers' annual decision-making in such a context,[48] demonstrating that until cereal prices levelled out in the mid-1890s the question of how much wheat should be planted was related to the trend of wheat prices over several years, rather than to the immediately contemporary and recently past situation and to the ratio of barley and wheat prices. The taking of a key decision depended on localised past experience, a method characteristic of most expressions of the farmers' point of view. Contemporary geographical comparison was more typical of the expert such as the civil servant or estate agent. A dichotomy between official and non-official views of the depression thus emerges. The former recognises, increasingly emphasises, regional variation, although the legislative response rarely possesses the geographical elements which would today be taken almost for granted in an agricultural policy; the latter focuses on present poverty compared to past prosperity *in situ*. It enabled broadly similar conclusions to be reached in very different circumstances: thus in Bedfordshire and Westmorland rather more than twice as many farms changed hands on average between 1879 and 1881 as between 1868 and 1871 despite the very considerable difference in types of farming and the impact of depression within the two counties.[49]

The individual farmer and the whole of Britain occupy opposite ends of the spectrum of the scale of incidence of depression. For the farmer what seemed to be was as important as the actuality of his position, but for Britain only the real situation had any meaning. For all its intricate regional variation, the depression's effect on Britain as a whole conformed to a broad spatial pattern, greatest in the cereal-growing lowland zone, least in the pastoral highland zone, mitigated in the vicinity of urban markets, heightened in more remote areas. At the other extreme the individual's experience was substantially, though not completely, independent of geography. It cannot be doubted that more farmers failed in some areas than others—in Suffolk than in Somerset, for example—but it is more important to recall that more farmers than usual failed in nearly every locality, and that in even the most depressed areas the majority survived for at least some years. Not a few made a good living in hard times

C

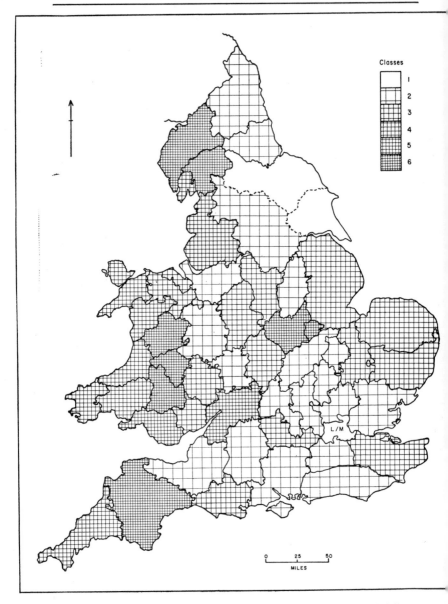

Fig 6 Agricultural failures, 1891–3 (a) in relation to agricultural failures, 1871–3 (b), (a/b): (1) less than 0·5; (2) 0·5 to less than 1·0; (3) 1·0 to less than 1·5; (4) 1·5 to less than 2·0; (5) 2·0 to less than 2·5; (6) more than 2·5. L/M, London and Middlesex

either on the basis of excellence within traditional orthodoxies, such as the Norfolk four-course, or by experiment and adaptation. The individual counted for more than the place or the period. It is thus scarcely surprising that even preliminary attempts to devise an index of the incidence of depression at the parish level and on the basis of 'farm sale' advertisements have revealed a high degree of local variation. Adjacent parishes with similar physical environments produce values of such indices over a very wide range,[50] supporting the view that at this level of generalisation the depression accentuated rather than weakened all kinds of local differences. Such variety of experience and practice, and the key role of the individual, were commented upon by Hall in 1913; [51] he also noted the seeming inexplicability and irrationality of much of the variation, such as rents in north Lancashire.[52] Nor was this variation restricted to agriculture, King and Arch making similar observations about village social life in 1913.[53]

At an intermediate level of generalisation—the county, the region, the greatest of estates—the importance of both individual and environment becomes important. Such authorities as Thompson and Perren have demonstrated the importance of the landlord,[54] his resources and his outlook, in creating differential experience of the depression. Perry and Johnston on the other hand have produced a trend-surface depression model at the county level which explains just over 40 per cent of the parish to parish variation in the incidence of depression in broadly environmental, locational and spatial terms. The other 60 per cent is to be ascribed to chance, and to spatially random factors such as landlord attitude and farmer skill.[55]

Although in many cases farmers were able in retrospect to look back to the mid-1870s as the great turning point towards depression, in their own and in the national experience, the onset of depression was not instantaneous. Nor was it well understood at the time, most commentators being inclined to look back on 1874[56] as the last of the good years and to 1874–5, when wheat prices fell 10s (50p) a quarter, as a sharp and uncomfortable break in prosperity. In fact many characteristic features of the depression can be traced back into the 1850s and 1860s, in the real if not always apparent profitability of livestock by comparison with grain, in the laying down of arable to permanent pasture, and in the increasing importance of fodder crops.[57]

Wheat prices, as has been noted, fell sharply in 1874 and 1875, but then hovered around 45s (£2.25) until 1883; of other agricultural prices only wool and cheese,[58] temporarily in 1879, fell sharply in the late 1870s and early 1880s. Yet this period is, and was, regarded as the first of the two most acute phases of depression, sufficient to warrant setting up the Richmond Commission. At the time adverse seasons were given most of the blame: 1875, 1877, 1878, 1879, 1881 and 1882 were all years of poor harvests, and 1879 was a disaster, rare in Britain, when almost every kind of farming was badly affected. 'The year 1879 marked the beginning of the end for the real old-time farmer, with his large numbers of labourers and easy-going life.'[59] There were notable regional exceptions such as the far north and the far west, but Tennyson was constrained to pessimistic comment in prefacing his brother's sonnets at the end of June:[60]

> Midnight—and joyless June gone by,
> And from the deluged park
> The cuckoo of a worse July
> Is calling thro' the dark

The importance of these difficult seasons lies in the continuing pre-eminence of cereal crops; there were still nearly 3 million acres of wheat in 1882. Poor seasons reduced yields and increased costs at a time when rents had reached a maximum and when overseas grain imports prevented prices from rising as they would formerly have done in such conditions.[61]

Farmers and landowners were inclined to blame the weather more than foreign competition during this first acute phase of depression;[62] and in public discussion such perennials as the rates, the railways, and the cost of education were aired.[63] The general opinion was that average seasons would restore modest prosperity and remove the disease problem. ' It would be against the known law of averages and against certain positive facts before them that they [prices] could possibly remain at the level they were at present.'[64] In fact the 1880s provided average or better than average seasons, relief from epidemics, but no more than a veneer of prosperity. During this decade prices fell across the whole of agriculture, and, more generally, so much so that 1885 rather than 1874 was often looked back on as the great turning point in the high-land zone, where lowland restocking after the liver fluke epidemic had lifted livestock prices early in the decade.[65] Particular localities had their own problems, such as the failure of root crops in Norfolk in 1887.[66] The belief that things would put themselves right persisted strongly, despite falling prices, until the mid-1880s; and as late as 1888 one writer could speak of more cheerful prospects.[67]

This cautious optimism, this absence of despondency in the face of falling prices, requires explanation. Average seasons doubtless played a part, though it is no surprise that they were less commended than the preceding poor seasons were condemned. Yields were more satisfactory after 1882,[68] the costs of production less inflated. The phenomenon of lower prices had by now become familiar, if unfriendly, and a body of practical experience in meeting the problem had been acquired. Landlords were continuing their policy of aid, revaluations and reduced rents augmenting the by now familiar remissions. On Thompson's estimate nominal rentals reached a peak in 1877 at 29s 9d (£1.49) per acre for England and Wales, and by 1885 their value had fallen to 24s 1d (£1.21).[69] Locally falls were more spectacular, in excess of 40 per cent near Lechlade by 1880.[70] The first intense phase of depression had also served to eliminate the weaker (as well as the shrewder) brethren, the idle and incompetent, the undercapitalised, perhaps in some cases the overcapitalised, and the profligate spenders.

The second acute phase of depression occupied the first half of the 1890s. Store cattle and wool prices fell sharply. wheat touching bottom at 22s 10d (£1.14) in 1894 and exceeding 30s (£1.50) only twice in the period 1893–1906. But by 1894 wheat was grown on less than 2 million acres. The droughts of 1892, 1893, 1895 and 1896 exacerbated the situation, particularly for the grazier and the dairy farmer, by now also facing foreign competition. Universally, however, prices were blamed. In the words of the knowledgeable Edward Stutt: 'I want better prices, that is the only thing that will make things right with us'.[71] Rents, and prices in general, had continued to fall: Thompson's figure for rent per acre was below 21s (£1.05) by 1896. The value of land (tithe included) assessed for income tax under Schedule A in Great Britain fell from £51 million in the late 1870s to £37 million at the turn of the century (Fig 7).[72] Only locally was there a complete collapse,

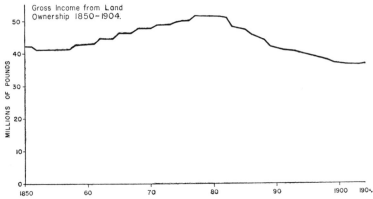

Fig 7   Gross income from land ownership 1850–1904 (Thompson, *JRSS* [1907], 614)

the best known and most conspicuous examples being in eastern Essex.[73] Elsewhere a diminished dependence on wheat, the increasing proportion of recently arrived tenants paying low rents and often accepting a low standard of living, and the unwillingness of most landowners to take land 'in hand', ensured at least that land was occupied, however unprofitably to all concerned. It was this second acute period of depression which received attention from the second Royal Commission.

Recovery was gradual but uneven. Wheat prices levelled out after 1896, but a book entitled *The Revival of English Agriculture* published in 1899 focused attention on horticulture and dairying, recognising the continuing problems of upland areas such as the Cotswolds, where there was little scope for innovation.[74] Diminished costs, rents which stayed down while prices rose slowly, and more basically gold discoveries in the Rand, were probably the main factors in the return of a modest prosperity; rents were often lower in the 1900s than the 1890s. The landlord, who had borne less than his due burden early in the depression, bore more later.[75] A number of farmers had entered the business on most favourable terms.[76] Hence eyewitnesses of the period before 1914 usually paint a picture of modest prosperity and stability in a framework of both traditional and innovational practice.[77]

There is then no single chronology for the depression. Changes in land use and in agricultural profitability began as early as the 1850s, two decades earlier than the sharp collapse in cereal prices which is usually thought of as epitomising the depression. The prices of livestock products fell later, less spectacularly but more erratically. Rents and capital values fell as a consequence of the fall in farm prices, and thus usually after them. The whole situation must be placed in a context of a generally falling price level.[78] Difficult seasons occurred early in the depression, accompanied by epidemics, and difficulties continued on a lesser scale and different in kind in the 1890s. These visible and immediate misfortunes and the experience of preceding years doubtless coloured the perception of those caught up in the depression, so that the late 1870s seemed particularly disastrous, and the 1880s often rather less so, despite more rapidly falling prices. Moreover men and methods as well as prices and profits changed; many of the farmers of the 1890s had never known prosperity, but they had accumulated some of the wisdom and experience of their predecessors. They acquired new means of meeting their problems, one typical instance being the use of basic slag as a grassland fertiliser.[79]

2

Causes of the Depression

PRICES

THE FALL IN prices in every branch of agriculture was the most conspicuous feature of the depression. The broad outline of what happened is quite clear: wheat and wool prices fell by half between the early 1870s and the mid-1890s, and cattle and sheep prices by one-quarter to one-third. Although the exact figures vary from market to market, from commentator to commentator, and according to the dates compared, and although at a more detailed level some considerable qualification of these broad trends is required, these falls cannot be disputed.

Cereal prices fell after two decades of agricultural prosperity during which they alone among agricultural prices had not risen strongly. The reality of the golden age was less remunerative and less profitable cereal farming.[1] The persistently downward trend in cereal prices begins early in the 1870s, and there were particularly sharp falls in 1874–5, 1883–4, and 1890–94 (Fig 8).[2] The price of barley and oats fell rather less sharply, the price differential between wheat and barley in particular diminishing to the extent of favouring barley in a few years. Not surprisingly some farmers responded by substituting barley or oats for wheat, and the acreage of these two cereals diminished much less rapidly than the wheat acreage.[3]

The cereal prices quoted are almost invariably derived from the official *London Gazette*; they are average values for sales

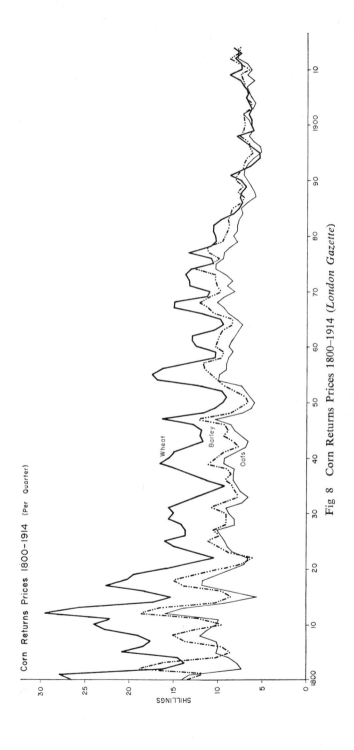

Corn Returns Prices 1800–1914 (Per Quarter)

SHILLINGS

Wheat

Barley

Oats

Fig 8   Corn Returns Prices 1800–1914 (*London Gazette*)

at the principal markets. Their relationship to reality was, as has been noted, commonly questioned even at the level of the weekly published price. It was suggested that the official price was too high, since samples of less than prime quality fetched lower prices, or were fed to livestock on the farm, and because during hard times many farmers were in a 'hand to mouth' situation where a quick sale at more or less any price was necessary.[4] Thus W. J. Malden recalled selling best wheat at 18s (90p) per quarter in 1893, for which year the average was 26s 4d. (£1.32).[5] In the early 1890s wheat was sold at 30s (£1.50) at some times of the year, and at 40s (£2) at others.[6] Conversely, however, enhanced seasonal fluctuations benefited other farmers, less likely to complain that the official price was misleading. Organised speculation to push up prices was important during both the 1880s and the late 1890s.[7] For barley growers there was always the possibility and objective of a malting sample which would command a good margin over the basic price.

Official prices thus show the trend of prices, an important factor in its own right, but individual experience in selling grain was on occasion very much better or very much worse than the average would suggest. Farmers were, however, for the most part agreed that prices were, to an increasing extent, too low to be profitable. Witnesses before the Richmond Commission in the early 1880s suggested as the minimum profitable price of wheat a range of values from 40s (£2) to 56s (£2.80), only a minority suggesting a figure below the average price for those years of 44s (£2.20) to 45s (£2.25). One witness ominously predicted the possibility of imports at 32s (£1.60), the level reached by the official price as early as 1886.[8]

In 1891 Primrose McConnell, one of the best known Essex Scots, could claim that wheat paid well at 30s (£1.50).[9] It would almost appear that by then low cereal prices were taken for granted, perhaps because of the decline in arable acreage, perhaps because of reduced costs and altered methods. Thus most farmers continued to grow some cereals; straw was a necessity, oats were still a highly remunerative crop near large towns,[10] and cereals could be fed to livestock should the price be unfavourable. No doubt less rational factors played a part in the survival of cereal cultivation at low prices—

FARMERS COULD LIVE THEN.

Value of Produce.—Oats, 17s. 6d. per qr. ; Barley, 23s. 6d. per qr. ; Wheat, 18s. 6d. per bag ; Cheese, 42s. 6d. per cwt.

FARMERS CAN'T LIVE NOW.

Value of Produce.—Oats, 26s. per qr. ; Barley, 45s. per qr. ; Wheat, 24s. per bag ; Cheese, 80s. per cwt.

The implication of this anti-farmer cartoon of 1880 is that high living rather than low prices is the root cause of the farmer's problems. The prices are inaccurate: wheat, for example, averaged 43s 10d (£2.19) in 1839 and 70s 8d (£3.53) in 1879

conservatism, ignorance, and the inability to finance a radical change in farming practice.[11]

Only one other agricultural commodity experienced a price collapse on a similar scale, and that was wool; but wool prices, unlike wheat prices, had been spectacularly high and wool growers unprecedently prosperous in earlier decades. The highest and lowest grades of wool were most severely affected, medium grades comparatively less. Lincoln wool fetched $25\frac{5}{8}$d (10·7p) per pound in 1872, and from $8\frac{1}{4}$d (3·4p) to $12\frac{3}{8}$d (5·1p) per lb between 1881 and 1900 (Fig 9). Scottish Blackface wool

Fig 9 Lincoln and Cheviot wool prices (per lb) 1870–1908 (Besse, *La crise et l'évolution d'agriculture en Angleterre*, 343, from official statistics)

averaged 11d (4·6p) per lb between 1860 and 1876, and 6d (2·5p) between 1880 and 1894, a loss of about 2s (10p) per beast yearly.[12] In Dorset, a county famous for both arable and grassland flocks, the loss on wool alone during this period was estimated at 10 guineas (£10.50) for every 100 acres.[13]

As a source of farm income wool was more important in the highland zone than in the lowland. To most farmers it was a secondary income; but even a loss of 2s (10p) an acre was keenly felt in hard times, and Thompson claims that falling wool prices upset the cost structure of arable high farming and led to the replacement of labour-demanding hurdled sheep, like the Hampshire Down, by less demanding grass breeds such as the Cheviot.[14] It is thus somewhat surprising that falling wool prices were not much commented upon during the depression; they were overshadowed by more conspicuous problems, notably disease.

'Wheat and wool are not everything.'[15] At the other extreme dairy prices, fresh milk prices in particular, fell very little. Various commentators estimated the fall in cheese and butter prices at between 10 and 30 per cent between the 1870s and the 1890s; the price of fresh milk fell rather less or not at all.[16] Certain places and periods were less fortunate; Garnett cited a halving of the price of Westmorland butter between 1874–5 and 1897,[17] and the late 1870s were particularly diffi-cult for cheese makers as imports increased, adverse seasons reduced milk yields, and market conditions deteriorated.[18]. In many respects milking and marketing, conditions of work and carriage, rather than prices were the dairy farmer's main prob-lems during this period.[19] The lucrative urban market, natur-ally protected, served to attract farmers into dairying from other branches of farming. Cheaper feeding stuffs were par-ticularly advantageous for the producer of winter milk at premium prices.[20]

The greatest uncertainty exists over livestock prices, notably because—as was universally agreed at the time—these were the most violently fluctuating agricultural prices. Moreover no official record of livestock prices comparable to the *London Gazette* cereal prices was kept; in so mobile a market it is hard to say how representative were prices from even the large London fatstock markets, let alone the numerous provincial store markets. Farmers were notoriously conservative and lackadaisical in their attitude towards selling livestock, a matter much discussed at the time,[21] and it is therefore also uncertain how large a part of recorded fat and store stock prices passed to the farmer, and how much to the dealer and other intermediaries. In this area there remains a need and scope for a great deal of regional research.

Fat cattle of prime quality fetched around 6s (30p) per lb in London in the mid-1870s and 4s 3d (21p) to 4s 6d (22p) 20 years later, a fall of 25–30 per cent (Fig 10). Fat sheep fell from 7s (35p) to around 5s 6d (27p) per lb during the same

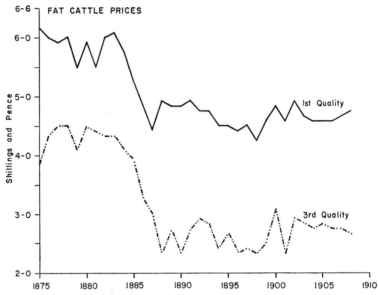

Fig 10   Fat cattle prices (per stone of 8lb live weight at London Metropolitan Meat Market) 1875–1908 (Besse, 341, from official statistics)

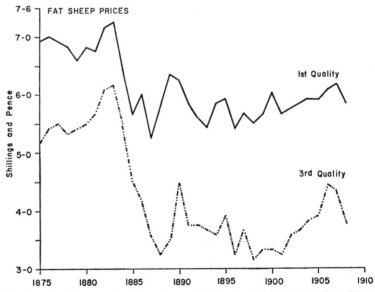

Fig 11   Fat sheep prices (per stone of 8 lb at London Metropolitan Meat
Market) 1875–1908 (Besse, 341–2, from official statistics)

period, a lesser fall but the sheep market was always more erratic (Fig 11). The price of store stock was more variable and the evidence is even more uncertain; one-year-old Teviotdale store cattle fetched about £9 10s 0d. (£9.50) in the mid-1870s and £8 in the mid-1890s, but for some years in the 1890s prices were much as in the 1870s, though on the other hand there were periods of catastrophic decline (Fig 12). Between 1883 and 1885, for example, lean beasts halved in price. By

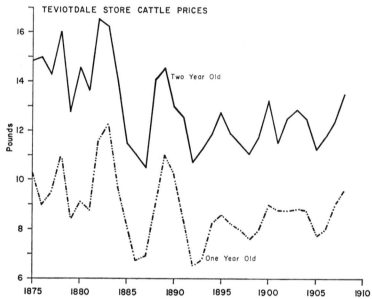

Fig 12 Teviotdale store cattle prices (average per head) 1875–1908
(Besse, 342, from official statistics)

selecting appropriate years and ignoring broader considerations it is possible to demonstrate almost any effect you please with respect to store cattle at this period. Throughout the depression, 1873–96, the average price of inferior cattle fell 1·63 per cent per annum, and that of prime cattle only 1·48 per cent.[22] As was also the case with sheep, imported meat was a strong competitor, mainly at the cheap end of the market.

Whereas cereal producers for the most part proclaimed the unprofitability of prices from early in the depression, livestock producers were less unanimous. The fall in livestock prices was less than the fall in prices in general, but the latter were not necessarily of much concern to the farmer. Wages remained high, although the labour force was reduced, and debts incurred during prior prosperity had to be paid off. Few rents, in pastoral districts in particular, fell by as much as 40 per cent, a broad approximation of the change in prices between the early 1870s and the mid-1890s.[23]

Whether the breeder and rearer in the hills or on poorer land or the feeding and fattening high farmer in the lowlands fared worse in the depression is another contentious issue. Fat-stock prices fell more than store prices; Besse suggests 20–40 per cent for beef in the period 1876–80 to 1904–08 and 8–12 per cent for stores during the same period.[24] Other commentators, but not all, emphasise the loss caused to feeder and fattener by the exclusion of foreign stores and the admission of frozen meat.[25] But the feeder was compensated by very considerable falls in the price of purchased feeding stuffs, maize falling by 45 per cent and cake by $37\frac{1}{2}$ per cent between 1867–71 and 1894–8.[26] Rents fell further and faster in the lowland zone. There was always scope for the fattener's traditional skill of turning cheap stores into dear meat. The breeder on the other hand was less favourably placed with respect to outgoings; he purchased little feed and pressure of population and demand for farms maintained high rents. The store market was more erratic than the meat market, and more outside the producer's control. Disease had more severe consequences for the breeder, and he had limited opportunity for diversification in many cases. If feeding kept the cereal producer going, if, as was claimed, it was his sheet-anchor,[27] the breeder had to resort to keeping more stock, already over-abundant in some areas, or accepting an even lower standard of living.

One commentator has suggested that between 1873 and 1893 gross farming returns fell on average by £2 per acre.[28] The ability of farmers to survive in such circumstances depended primarily on their willingness and ability to economise, to make changes, or to live off their reserves.

Those affected by falling prices were generally more inclined to comment on their impact than to explore their antecedents. In any event early commentators, inside and outside farming, regarded circumstances of production, such as adverse seasons,

Page 49

A Herefordshire silo built in 1885, a not uncommon innovation of the period but one which was often soon given up.

(*above*) Glasshouses and bungalow at Rew, Martinstown, Dorchester, built c 1890 by Alfred Dight and still in use in 1972. One of the few smallholdings in the scheme to succeed; (*below*) a smallholder's bungalow built c 1890 at Rew, Martinstown, Dorchester; photographed 1972. Constructed of timber, brick and corrugated iron by the first occupier of an 8 acre holding, it has been little altered in 80 years

rather than low prices as their basic problem. It is, however, scarcely to be doubted that falling prices were the real issue. They reflected the ability of several areas of European settlement in the Americas and Australasia to make a good living by providing large quantities of cheap and wholesome food for the British market (Fig 13). Where there were few or no imports, potatoes and fresh milk, for example, prices fell very little. The absence of tariffs gave the foreign or colonial producers free access to an affluent and expanding British market. What circumstances made it possible for their prices persistently to undercut the British farmer?

Some of the overseas farmer's costs of production, most notably labour in newly settled areas, were higher than in Britain, but there is plenty of evidence pointing to his willingness to work harder for a lower return than his British counterpart. The primary advantage was cheap land, often of high virgin fertility, itself the lure of many migrants under such legislation as the US Homestead Acts, and even in areas where there was some tradition of a relatively high price for land, as in New Zealand. Not only was land cheap, but it was becoming more accessible. There were 9,021 miles of railway in the USA in 1850, 52,922 miles (and peace restored) by 1870.[29] Access to markets also improved: it cost $2\frac{1}{2}$d (1p) per lb to ship mutton from New Zealand to Britain in 1882, but only a halfpenny (0·2p) per lb in 1898.[30] To move wheat from Chicago to Liverpool cost 15s 11d (80p) per quarter in the late 1860s, but only 3s 11d (20p) in the early 1900s.[31] This fall accounts for about half the fall in wheat prices in Britain during this period. 'The age was engaged in annihilating distance.'[32] These circumstances—extended railways, and improved steamers, more cheaply and more efficiently operated—enabled twice as much grain to be imported into Britain in the early 1900s as in the early 1870s (Fig 13). The terms of trade moved against the European agricultural producer.

These agricultural exports came from areas not only of British settlements but also of substantial British investment during this epoch when Britain's commercial and technical pre-eminence was greatest. These were areas with British-owned railways and banks, markets for British machines and manufactures. Wheat, wool, beef and butter were the main

D

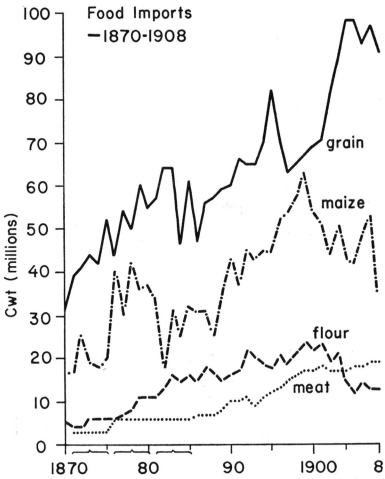

Fig 13   British food imports 1870–1908 (Besse, 365, 377, 382–3, from official statistics)

commodities with which these pioneer societies could service this British investment and buy British exports. This remains a major role of their pastoral industries, in New Zealand, for example, in the 1970s. Agricultural exports were then a necessity to both the pioneer settler and the British investor and exporter.

The demographic and technological causes of falling prices, and the commercial circumstances of increased food imports, must also be understood in their general economic context of deflation. Gold discoveries in the 1850s and 1860s had financed the rising prices and economic expansion of these decades; the absence of such discoveries, the relative scarcity of gold, in the expanding commercial world depressed prices, and not merely agricultural prices, by as much as 40 per cent in Britain between the early 1870s and the mid-1890s. It has been suggested that the South African gold discoveries were one factor in the amelioration of agricultural distress at the end of the nineteenth century.[33] This general economic context received not inconsiderable discussion before the Royal Commission of 1893–5, usually in the form of debate on bimetallism (ie coinage of silver as well as gold) as a means of countering the deflation induced by a shortage of gold. Ten commissioners, and many witnesses, favoured bimetallism, but the Commission's influential economist, Giffen, argued against the step on the reasonable grounds that the rise in prices which it might be expected to produce would not assist farmers.[34]

A third group of factors depressing prices originated within Britain; less important than external conditions they were nevertheless much discussed. Bad farming weather reduced the quality as well as the yield of cereals, and livestock disease commonly had the same effect, although it was possible to fatten or 'coathe' rotted sheep even in 1879, thus reducing losses.[35] The policy of excluding foreign store cattle has already been mentioned. A parallel and more justifiable complaint was that the grassing down of arable land had meant that farmers could fatten more stock in summer while making possible no increase in the stock that could be carried through the winter. The consequence was high store prices in spring, and low store and fat-stock prices in autumn.[36] These were essentially complaints as to margins rather than prices, from livestock producers in arable districts. Although the cash price of beef and mutton fell during the depression, its purchasing power increased in response to the sustained and increased urban demand for meat.[37] By comparison the demand for wheat was relatively inelastic despite falling prices and increased purchasing power. Consumer preference—and the consumer's increasing financial ability to choose and prefer—was thus a further not unimportant factor in determining the extent to which prices fell, increasing the impact of depression on different branches of agriculture.

SEASONS AND SICKNESS

Whatever were the basic causes of the depression, those most closely caught up in it were strongly inclined to stress the part played by adverse seasons and livestock disease until at least the mid-1880s. Only when the depression was well advanced was there general awareness that the seasons were of marginal significance, not least because the summers of the 1890s were less exceptional and generally more acceptable than those of the late 1870s and early 1880s. Complaints of adverse seasons were widespread, only a few peripheral areas in the north and west like Cornwall and the Scottish Highlands having less cause for complaint.[38] Within the districts substantially affected, a high degree of local variation resulted from such matters as the geology of the area, the state of the drains and the attitude of the individual farmer or landowner.

NOT SUCH DISAGREEABLE WEATHER FOR THE HAYMAKERS
AS SOME PEOPLE THINK.

Punch's comment on the summer of 1879

The farmer certainly had cause to complain about the weather, and it was no mere amplification of the countryman's proverbial propensity to grumble about it that made itself heard. Between 1873 and 1882 only two summers were warmer than the 20 year average.[39] The situation was such as to draw forth expert opinion supporting farmers' complaints. Caird commented: 'Until we have had a succession of good seasons we cannot contemplate anything else but a period of low farming.'[40] Professor Voelcker of the Royal Agricultural College thought that bad weather had done more mischief than anything else to the agricultural community.[41] By contrast, dry summers, a feature of the later depression years of 1884, 1885, 1887, 1892, 1893, 1895 and 1896, received much less contemporary comment than their ill-favoured precursors.

The most immediately conspicuous effect of cool and wet summers was on cereal crops. Harvests were belated—in 1879 the wheat harvest in Bedfordshire began early in September, over a month later than usual[42]—protracted, and costly of labour. One farmer estimated that in 1877 the harvest cost £200 more than usual, nullifying his attempts to economise on labour.[43] Moreover quality and yields were usually poor in such circumstances; between 1879 and 1882 wheat yields were

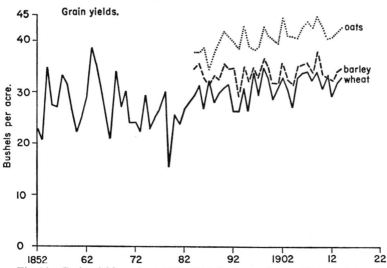

Fig 14   Grain yields: wheat 1852–1914, barley and oats 1884–1914 (Venn, *Agricultural Economics*, 555–6)

every year below the 10 year moving mean, in 1879 for the United Kingdom as a whole by 9·7 bushels per acre (Fig 14). In Shropshire cereal yields were down by half.[44] The effect on quality cannot be so succinctly stated, but it was undoubtedly a secondary factor in reducing grain prices and in reducing the proportion of the crop which the producer was prepared to offer for sale.[45] To some extent adverse seasons had a cumulative effect: wet years were weedy years, a succession of such years making weed control—an integral part of high farming—impossible, particularly on heavy land where the traditional method of bare fallow failed in this role in wet seasons.[46] Labour economies aggravated this state of affairs and comments on the foul state of the land were commonplace by the late 1870s: the Duke of Bedford's agent wrote of farms 'one mass of couch . . . full of docks and noxious weeds'[47] and Richard Jefferies wrote of 'weeds . . . so thick that even a pheasant can hide'.[48]

In some localities the state of the drains was a further problem. The succession of wet years made it only too evident that the tile drains laid in the early high farming years which followed the technical and legislative developments in draining of the 1840s had reached the end of their useful life. They were expected to last 15–25 years, but in many instances they had been poorly laid and indifferently maintained.[49] The summer of 1879 appears as a last straw in this context, triggering off a renewed emphasis and activity. As much public drainage money was applied for in the period November 1879 to February 1880 as in the whole period 1876–8.[50] Some landlords offered new drains as an alternative to reduced rents, or drained in the hope of sustaining rents or even finding tenants, but as prices fell not all could continue this policy.[51] Drainage, however, remained an area where even in the worst times shrewd men, like Strutt,[52] were prepared to spend money if they could.

Cool and wet summers had less immediately conspicuous, but possibly more lasting, effects in grassland districts. Superficially all was well, for drought rather than rain was the traditional enemy of grazier and dairyman; so much was this the case that some contemporary commentators, Little and Coleman, for example, felt that it was particularly important to draw attention to grassland difficulties.[53] Grass grew in such summers, but less nutritious and palatable species tended to gain and hold a dominant position, reducing the capacity of such pastures to fatten stock. In Bedfordshire 'grass farmers to a man told how sadly the pastures were damaged'.[54] In some instances this took place very quickly; by 1881 the value of some meadows in the Thames valley had fallen from £3 to 10s (50p) per acre.[55] It was because deterioration tended to be permanent in the prevailing economic conditions that Little and others gave the matter such emphasis.

The most conspicuous effect of adverse seasons on pastoral farming was, however, indirect, through the increased incidence of disease. Cattle disease had become an acute problem in the mid-1860s, when epidemics of pleuro-pneumonia and rinderpest occurred. These hastened the demise of the urban dairy, fostered government action on veterinary matters—notably, if rather vacillatingly, on livestock imports—and brought into existence an important farmer's organisation, the Central Chamber of Agriculture. Pleuro-pneumonia is thought to have killed 100,000 cattle between 1869 and 1894;[56] disease in general disrupted markets and impeded the increasingly important export of stud stock.[57] Crops as well as stock were affected, potato blight—characteristically a disease of cool wet summers—administering the *coup de grace* to many small potato growers in the Fens in the early 1880s.[58]

How far these diseases were related to climatic conditions is generally uncertain, and their occurrence was sporadic. By comparison liver fluke, or 'rot', was undoubtedly favoured by cool wet summers, reaching the scale of an epidemic in 1879–81. The water snail, which is the fluke's host at one phase of its life cycle, lived in the cold damp grasslands and was always a threat;[59] in such conditions as prevailed between 1879 and 1881 it thrived, killing about 10 per cent of all sheep, a loss estimated at between £10 and £12 million.[60] A few counties largely escaped—Cornwall was one—but most did not; mortality exceeded 20 per cent in some counties, notably Devonshire, and was higher in the worst affected parishes.[61] In Babcary, Somerset, eighty sheep survived out of 2,500.[62] Generally high rainfall areas and the poorly drained localities within the lowland zone were worst affected. There were minor consolations; rotted sheep could be fattened (or 'coathed') if their condition were detected soon enough, reducing but not eliminating the loss. The upland breeder had no such consolation, his loss being absolute—witness the high incidence of agricultural bankruptcy in central Wales in the early 1880s[63]—but the subsequent years of lowland restocking were to his profit. The general uncertainty and unpredictability of the disease problem, liver fluke and otherwise, compounded difficulties, inhibiting decision making, discouraging desirable diversification into grassland farming, and undermining the farmer's credit.[64] Liver fluke had important long-term effects: the great epidemic was still being talked about in the 1890s[65] and was undoubtedly an important secondary factor in the decline of lowland sheep numbers in the late nineteenth century.

The run of dry summers in the 1890s, as we have said, received less comment than the earlier spell of wet years. By this time their peripheral role in the crisis was recognised; they fostered no devastating diseases, they facilitated weed control, and they were inherently enjoyable. Most but not all dry summers reduced cereal yields, but at least such a harvest was quick and cheap, if unrewarding. The effects on livestock were usually more conspicuous, graziers and dairy farmers being put in a difficult position; for in such years the fattener usually limited his purchase of stores, thus transferring the real burden to the breeder.

Adverse seasons affected different systems and localities in different ways, but only the most fortunate farmer completely escaped their effects between 1870 and 1900. Most commentators singled out clay farms, arable or grass, as most severely affected by wet seasons, which raised costs and reduced productivity; within this category distinctions could profitably be made. Little, for example, singled out the Oxford Clay and the Lias in his report on the southern and western counties in 1882.[66] In cold years the uplands were affected almost regardless of soil type, and this may be a secondary reason why the frontiers of cultivation retreated in some districts during the depression. However, reclamation was still being actively pursued in some northern areas in the 1880s.[67] In dry years some heavy arable could be difficult, but on upland soils the limestone and the chalk were the worst affected. Hence their slow recovery from the mid-1890s. Although new machinery from the USA had done something to help the heavy land cultivator,[68] the farmer remained late in the nineteenth century very largely shackled by his environment. Heavy clays were regarded unfavourably because costs of cultivation made them unprofitable save in optimal seasons; light land produced miserable crops in dry years. It is therefore scarcely surprising that the environment, its stable and its transient elements, and the success or failure of farmers should display so many correlations, direct and indirect. Everyone agreed that the farmers whose land was a fertile well drained loam was better placed than most to face difficult circumstances, whatever the weather and whatever his farming system.[69]

Difficult seasons, epidemic and endemic disease, made things harder for the farmer, but they were not the prime cause of depression. Nevertheless, if the farmer's conception of his economic interests was many times misplaced, it is of obvious significance for the way in which we analyse his condition and behaviour. If the farmer thought the seasons were the main problem—and there is evidence that until as late as the mid-1880s most of them did—it was such misperceptions rather than the reality he failed to comprehend which determined his course of action. In retrospect this phenomenon itself was recognised, as 'the complete failure of agricultural experts to recognise at the beginning of the period the permanent character of the various forces then at work'.[70] An obsession with the weather had obscured consideration of other matters, fostering a view that fundamental changes would be premature and that in time normal seasons—whatever that might mean—would put matters right.[71]

It remains a little surprising that this attitude survived the experience of the 1870s, when the established tendency of cereal prices to compensate the farmer in poor seasons failed to act; no doubt mere wishful thinking and inertia were also important. Acceptance of the need for fundamental changes was thus delayed, perhaps by more than a decade. This delay was to make changes harder to accomplish, since the farmers' financial position was continuously weakened during the period.[72] It is interesting, and by no means idle, to speculate as to what effects a more determined movement towards diversification in general, and grassland farming in particular, in the 1870s might have had on the course of depression.

SOME SCAPEGOATS AND SECONDARY CAUSES

There remain to be discussed a number of secondary causes of the depression and a number of scapegoats. Contemporary writers were almost as prone to exaggerate these as they were to ignore or overlook the real issues. This reflects not only the political impossibility of a return to protection, but the fact that these secondary causes were commonly local or even individual, and not necessarily novel. What the farmer and landowner had accepted and borne in good times became a burden in hard times, the more readily identifiable as such because it was already familiar.[73] Legislative action to counter the depression took place largely in this area—the Agricultural Holdings Acts of 1875 and 1883, and the Rating Act of 1896, for example—even though it was apparent from an early period that such action could be no more than palliative. By the 1890s even such limited benevolence angered some farmers. In the words of one Lincolnshire farmer: 'We want no more law. If we can't have better prices the next best thing for the farmer is to close the House of Commons for ten years'.[74] But such exasperation did not stop numerous farmers from discussing a wide range of secondary issues, such as rates and taxes, high rents, and methods of selling.

There never has been a time when property owners have failed to complain about taxation, local and national; the late nineteenth century was no exception. So much was this the case, and so contentiously was the topic discussed by the second Royal Commission, that it led indirectly to the resignation of the chairman, to a minority report, a number of reservations, and an abundance of ill-feeling.[75] The 'burden on the land', the contemporary euphemism for rates, taxes, and tithe, was a favourite topic of witnesses and submissions to both commissions, as was the related issue of how helpful derating of farm land would be to agriculture. Although Shaw-Lefevre demonstrated that rates had diminished, the

"THE HORSE AND THE LOADED ASS."

" A MAN WHO KEPT A HORSE AND AN ASS WAS WONT IN HIS JOURNEY TO SPARE THE HORSE AND PUT ALL THE BURDEN UPON THE ASS'S BACK."
[*See Right Hon. H-nry Ch-pl-n's edition of "Æsop's Fables"—to be continued.*]

This cartoon refers to the Agricultural Rating Bill of 1896. 'Squire' Chaplin appears as the farmer's and landowner's friend, but note the continuing anti-agricultural bias of *Punch*. Why is the country the large horse and the town the small ass?

majority of his fellow Royal Commissioners disagreed.[76] But all did recognise that rates were heavier in the more depressed lowland zone and that their incidence reflected neither ability to pay nor the usefulness of the services they went to support. It was such characteristics rather than the basic issue of increase or decrease which made these matters so contentious; moreover the incidence of such payments, in cash and not easily postponed, must be related to the diminishing income of the agricultural community.[77] 'There is a great cry that rates are high, but I believe that this is due rather to the increased difficulty of paying the rates.'[78] Apparent irrationality and unpredictability exacerbated the situation. The valuations on which rates were based generally diminished, and comparative lists making this clear are commonplaces of the assistant commissioners' reports to the second Royal Commission. But the individual landlord who had legitimately favoured rent remission, perhaps selectively, over rent reduction received no such rate relief.[79] Maxton observed that in Scotland the payment of local taxes took 6·8 per cent of landowners' rental income in 1872, 7·1 per cent in 1892 and 9 per cent in 1913–14, a very small increase in a time of generally increasing taxation.[80] The 'burden on the land' argument was evidently pressed out of all proportion to its significance, a phenomenon in itself of some importance for an understanding of contemporary attitudes and perceptions.

High rents were an issue in two respects. A minority of farmers, mainly in the north and west, claimed that rents had not fallen sufficiently, and that landowners were not bearing a sufficient and fair share of agriculture's misfortunes.[81] A few even argued for intervention on Irish lines, for the three 'Fs' of fair rent, fixity of tenure, and free sale, but this was rejected by the Royal Commission of the 1890s. Characteristically such complaints came from areas where non-agricultural issues exacerbated landlord and tenant relationships, such as Wales, and from areas where the depression had its most minimal impact, such as Lancashire. Security of tenure was also an issue in such districts. Certainly rents dropped after prices had dropped, as might *a priori* be expected,[82] but the evidence suggests that only exceptionally were rents not reduced. Where this was the case, the farmers were often primarily responsible through their willingness to offer high rents when farms came on the market.

A general discussion of the course of rents before and during the depression characterised a much wider group than the radical anti-landlord party. Most agreed that an unfortunate consequence of a generation of prosperity had been to encourage inexperienced tenants to take farms at rents which were too high and in the case of arable farms with too little capital to withstand a run of bad seasons.[83] However, it takes two to make a contract, and the willingness of some landlords to play their part in this situation must be noted. In the highland zone letting farms by tender had similar unfortunate results. In some cases the successful urban businessman was the culprit, but elsewhere rural overpopulation was the prime cause, a fact favouring migration and emigration.[84] In a few areas special circumstances prevailed: returning Cornish miners were ready to pay quite ridiculous prices, a farm near Helston being rented at £115 on changing hands in 1881 when formerly it had fetched £40.[85] It is scarcely surprising that where such circumstances prevailed, landowners were in no haste to reduce rents; in fact some reductions and remissions were more a return to rationality from a situation where greed and ignorance had inflated rents than a simple response to the depression.

The depression then drew the attention of farmers and landowners to old issues in their relationship which had become new problems. Tenant right became an issue of some significance, not because it had never previously been considered but because depression generated an increased turnover of farmers, forced even more to examine what their position would be if they decided to leave, and made some wish to diversify into areas such as fruit growing, in which long-term tenant investment, and thus tenant right, was quite fundamental.[86] As late as the 1890s some tenants were required strictly to follow the four-course rotation,[87] a barrier to any flexibility, but more often depression enabled tenants to obtain a better and freer bargain. The creditworthiness of the farmer was affected not only by general commercial conditions —the Glasgow Bank failed spectacularly in 1878—but by the law of distress, which put the landowner in a privileged position over other creditors, again a matter of importance in hard times, and without which even more farmers would have failed.[88] Landlords generally favoured this situation, though tradesmen did not, and farmers were divided, some arguing for abolition as a stimulus to a truly commercial and competitive outlook, others for its continuance as a minor restraint on complete collapse. Evidently if not all farmers loved their landlord, almost all distrusted their trade creditors. As one Lincolnshire farmer put it: 'The tenant [had] much better fall into his landlord's hands than anyone else's'.[89]

Methods of selling appear, superficially at least, as a less important though again a perennial issue. The farmers' attitude towards, and behaviour during, market day has always been criticised. Singled out for comment during the depression was the farmer's almost universal insistence on the superiority and infallibility of his own visual judgement in buying and selling livestock.[90] It was easy to demonstrate that the butcher and the dealer, daily buyers and sellers, were usually much more skilful, but the weighbridge offended the farmer's pride and his adversary's purse, and when installed was little used. The issue may seem a trivial one, but it serves well to illustrate the stubborn irrationality and conservatism of a large number of farmers, and on one estimate this method of selling cost farmers almost £7 million, an average of £25 each, in 1888.[91] In fact many farmers ceased to be active in the markets in the traditional sense during this period; on the one hand a number of farms came to be occupied by stock owned by dealers,[92] and on the other hand the regular auction market increasingly ousted the old and occasional fairs and the itinerant dealer. During this period many of the names which today appear in the sale columns of country newspapers commonly first appeared in the role of auctioneer.[93]

Wages were a cause of complaint on the simple grounds that they always had been, and that they fell much less sharply than prices or rents. Between 1878 and 1888, for example, prices fell 21·5 per cent, labour costs 6 per cent.[94] Significantly such complaints were less typical of Scotland than of lowland England, with its established tradition of cheap labour inefficiently used.[95] In fact, as Ojala has demonstrated, the productivity of farm labour rose by almost one-fifth between the late 1860s and the late 1890s.[96] The farmer economised by employing less labour much more than by reducing wages, a major reason for the conversion of arable to pasture during this period.[97]

A host of other issues was argued about, so much so that an exhaustive list is almost inconceivable, but we can mention such hardy perennials as the game laws, the adulteration of fertilisers and feeding stuffs, railway rates, and the diminishing fertility of virgin marginal land brought into cultivation in mid-century. All mattered, some were legislated upon, and most highlight some facet of the limitations of the knowledge and outlook of the agricultural interest (railway rates, for example). As has been mentioned, such areas of concern were characteristically of local, particular, and not necessarily novel, impact, rather than fundamental and widespread causes whose disappearance would have caused the depression to disappear also. It remains true that neither these issues nor the basic causes appear to have been particularly well understood by many of those involved.

One fundamental matter remains for discussion—the slow pace at which necessary adjustments were made, particularly by farmers. There was a great reluctance to clamber out of the rut which had been so comfortable in the 1850s and 1860s. As early as 1875 two advocates of grassing down commented: 'Many persons are the servants not the masters of their farms'.[98] The assistant commissioner who toured the Yorkshire Wolds in 1881 observed: 'A radical alteration of system appears necessary, yet I could not find that much had been done by way of experiment'.[99] In this sense the rich rewards of mid-century high farming were a basic cause of the depression, the reason why the cereal acreage diminished relatively slowly and why farmers reversed this trend so readily as soon as prospects improved.

It is easy to suggest many reasons why changes were slow— the increasing financial weakness of agriculture, bad seasons and the incidence of disease early in the depression, and the tendency, scarcely to be criticised, for farmers to react to trends in prices rather than short-term movements, at least in the downward direction[100]—and it is only too easy to view the whole situation with the hindsight of the 1970s, forgetting the intellectual and geographical isolation of the farmer, his limited education and his limited expectation of action from central and local government. Reaction was slow, but it is not inconceivable that speedier response might considerably have eased the situation; in particular, appropriate action to foster diversification in arable districts might well have assisted the agricultural interest without damaging the national well-being. This is presumably what Astor and Rowntree had in mind in suggesting that 'appropriate measures of assistance would have eased their position without any prejudice to the national welfare'.[101] The reimposition of protection was as yet unthinkable, and in Europe it served merely to defer difficulties which have re-emerged as the 'structural problem' of the 1970s. What a succession of governments offered the depressed agricultural interest was a series of palliatives, perhaps as strong a degree of agricultural intervention as even the farmers would have accepted.

(*above*) Claxton's Barn, Rew, Martinstown, Dorchester, built c 1890; photographed 1972. General merchants as well as smallholders, the Claxton's required a large barn. Note use of corrugated iron, and abandonment of local and traditional materials, in the main building; but the lean-to at the rear is of flint and chalk (see p 104): (*below*) Ballarat Farm, Rew, Martinstown, Dorchester, built c 1890; photographed 1972. As the name suggests, the builder and first occupier of the holding was a prosperous returned goldminer. The house is untypically large and substantial for a smallholding of the period (see p 104)

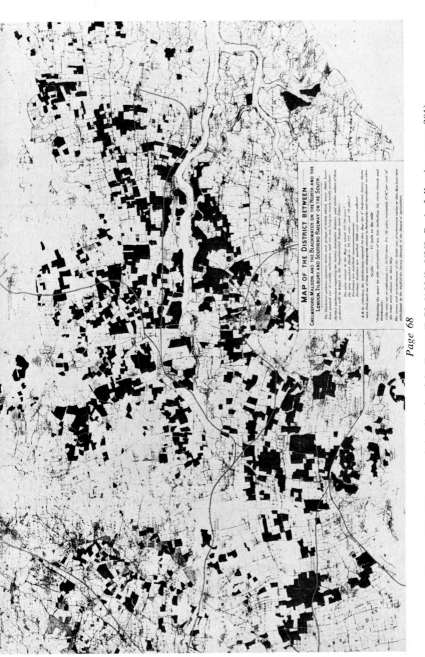

Hunter Pringle's map of derelict land in Essex (RC2 [1894], XVI, Pt 1, following page 801):
'The blackened portions represent fields and groups of fields which, since 1880, have passed
out of arable cultivation and are now lying in coarse, weedy pastures' (see p 85)

Landowners and the Depression

THE MISFORTUNES OF agriculture were widespread and persistent in their effects, but three groups—landowners, farmers, and farm workers—were directly involved. Among these the landowner was probably the most severely affected in relative terms, although he generally remained better off than most farmers and all labourers. A class owning almost 90 per cent of the land[1] and including its most powerful families and its most ancient institutions was not, however, in such a position as to command—nor did it generally seek—public sympathy. Rather the landowner was to an increasing extent a political 'Aunt Sally', in England and Scotland as much as in Wales and Ireland. 'Three acres and a cow', a characteristically Victorian view of Utopia, is also an attack on landowners.[2] Most appear to have accepted their economic and social misfortunes stoically, and many had sources of income other than the land.[3] Personal relationships with tenants remained for the most part good although there were regional exceptions and some deterioration late in the period.[4] Nevertheless the depression made demands on landowners—on their energy and adaptability if they were keenly interested in running their estates, on their patience if they were not, and on their purse regardless of their attitudes.

RENTS

The heart of the matter for the landowner was that to an increasing extent tenants could not, or would not, pay the

E

rent. Almost every aspect of this phenomenon is so well documented in estate archives, and in public discussion of the depression, that its importance has at times been exaggerated. As a problem distinct from that of the minority of chronically insolvent or reluctant tenants it first appears early in the 1870s;[5] it was commonly posed in the form of a polite request by the tenant for a reduction, or of a notice of intention to quit. This latter was not necessarily to be taken at its face value; as often as not it was a euphemistically sharp way of calling for a lower rent.[6]

The landlord could respond in several ways. In some localities, from some landowners and early in the depression, refusal was not uncommon: 'I shall give no relief to my tenants, I cannot afford it; and sooner than the rent shall be reduced it shall grow thorns and thistles'.[7] It did! And the owner eventually reached a more realistic appreciation of what he could and could not afford. There were evictions in a few areas,[8] but generally landowners soon came to see that their tenants had real problems which deserved assistance. And that new tenants would be hard to come by. Thus agents were instructed to keep tenants, or to let farms 'to whoever would come to work it',[9] a policy which in some cases persisted throughout the depression. Most landowners preferred this policy to facing the risks and costs of entering farming on their own account in such difficult times.

Early in the depression the tenant was usually offered a remission or abatement of rent rather than a permanent reduction, which came later in the depression, when its permanence was accepted and necessary revaluations were executed.[10] Remissions and abatements were not, however, wholly satisfactory and often they came too late; they put the farmer in a position of continuing uncertainty, and did not reduce the rateable value.[11] If, as usually happened, they were granted to all tenants other than those in arrears or under notice, they helped the worthless as well as the worthy;[12] and if selective, they made for social disharmony, as when new tenants were favoured over old, or at worst favoured the least competent.[13]

Landlord policy was at times an erratic 'combination of benevolence . . . with unsound economic practice'.[14] Orr cites one Oxfordshire case where the rent of an 800 acre farm was

THE AGRICULTURAL INTEREST.

Landlord (to Tenant who had given up Farming at the end of his Lease, to await better times). "WELL, JACKSON, HOW DO YOU LIKE LIVING ON YOUR CAPITAL?"

Farmer. "NOT TOO WELL, MY LORD; BUT I FIND IT CHEAPER THAN LETTING YOU LIVE ON IT!"

This well known Punch cartoon appeared in August 1879. At this date prices had fallen, rents had not. Note the reference to a lease, and the indication that shrewd men left farming early in the depression

not adjusted between 1879 and 1883, when, having fallen vacant, it was let at 10s (50p) per acre, though the previous tenant had been told that such a rent was outrageous. The farm was then divided and rents reduced to 8s (40p), despite expenditure on buildings. The owner had had enough and proceeded to sell the farm to an owner who pursued a policy of extreme economy.[15] In Scotland a generous policy reputedly had the effect of making tenants offer rents which they could afford in only the best years, an unsatisfactory situation from everyone's point of view.[16] On the whole farmers disliked the uncertain and arbitrary generosity of a policy of remission; landlords were aware of this, but also of its useful flexibility. The necessary long-term measure of revaluation and reduction was preferred by the tenant, but the owner saw that method, although it engendered a lower rateable value, as a slow, not inexpensive, and almost irreversible process. This is not to say that rents could never be raised or that landlords long continued to hold an ephemeral view of the character of the depression; but social pressure and custom made it relatively difficult to raise a sitting tenant's rent,[17] and so a reduction was an acceptance of a potentially long-term diminution of income, particularly should the state of farming get better and the turnover of tenants diminish.

Arrears were another aspect of the problem. In practice they were almost unavoidable, building up in the two periods of most severe depression either to be written off or to be reduced in better times. On the Wilton estate accumulated arrears reached 80 per cent of the rental, and on individual farms in the West of England they attained 2 years' rental by the early 1880s.[18] Little noted how quickly this took place: on one estate nine tenants were in arrears in 1876, but there were thirty-six in 1878.[19] Pringle suggests a similar situation in Axholme in the early 1890s.[20] These examples suggest over-renting, but arrears of half a year's rent were commonplace. Only a few landlords fixed their rents in terms of corn prices, following an ancient custom.[21] Finally there was the possibility of maintaining rents but increasing landlord investment, in drainage, in new buildings, in grassing down, for example, an excellent attitude in many respects but beyond the means of most owners for more than a few years.[22]

Faced with so many alternatives most landlords pursued a pragmatic policy. Only a few, like Lord Wantage, specified their objectives, and his was 'to keep tenants on their legs'.[23] It was impossible to prevent some tenants from leaving, but the agent could be encouraged to favour the best over the worst, the merely unfortunate over the clearly incompetent. Only the lucky landowner, at least in the lowland zone, could escape having some farms unlet at some periods, but this might be better than accepting a nominal rent from a bad tenant. In the last resort some farms were let rent-free to avoid the expense of taking them 'in hand'.[24] Appropriate advertisement might be tried as a means of attracting energetic Scots or Westcountrymen. Remissions would reflect short-term trends, reduction long-term policy. Considerable economies in estate and personal expenditure were commonplace unless the landowner had other sources of income,[25] but land would only be sold in the last resort because its value was so much reduced.

At this point exemplification is appropriate. In a book published in 1897 the Duke of Bedford told of his experience on the Thorney and Woburn estates—perhaps authorship was another kind of agricultural diversification! At Thorney there were remissions in 1879, 1880, 1881, and 1882, and every year from 1885 to 1895. These ranged from 10 per cent of the year's rent in 1888 to an entire half-year's rent in 1885. Remissions were not granted to those who had given or received notice to quit, but were not otherwise selective. From 1879 to 1895 the total remission was £145,911, about six times the nominal 1895 rental, or more than four times the nominal 1878 rental. In some years arrears built up, but they were never more than a few thousand pounds, small by comparison with many other properties. Finally there were two revaluations—a reduction of 10 per cent in 1881 and of 35 per cent in 1895. (This latter was carried out by W. C. Little.)[26] At Chicksands in Bedfordshire a half-yearly rent roll of £2,619 in 1872 had become £1,450 by 1888.[27]

Since religion and politics exacerbated landlord-tenant relationships in Wales, the situation there was thoroughly examined, by a Royal Commission and in abundant and often partisan literature. One book[28] has an appendix which gives details of rents, reductions, and abatements on a large number of North Wales estates. The first impression is of enormous variability: Lord Stanley, an Anglesey landowner, disapproved of remission in principle, but his estate had not been revalued during the century; on the same island Sir George Meyrick remitted on seven occasions between 1883 and 1896, but he gave no permanent reduction, and had revalued, presumably upwards, in 1871. These are instances from a partisan pro-landlord book; most of the examples show that in general landowners gave some help, though not on the scale of the Thorney estate in a much more severely depressed area. In many cases, however, very little is said of the sharp increases in rent during the first three-quarters of the century, reputedly characteristic of Wales.

Certainly rents had risen, in Wales almost doubling since 1815,[29] and in Wichwood Forest (Oxfordshire) certainly increasing by more than 60 per cent since 1851.[30] For England and Wales Caird gave an estimate of no more than 21 per cent for the period 1857–75, and another authority 28 per cent for a similar but slightly longer period.[31] There were three main causes of this increase: agriculture prospered in the 1850s and 1860s; there was substantial landlord investment in drainage, building and reclamation,[32] and there was continuous demand for farms while agriculture remained so evidently profitable, not only from the agricultural but also from the business community.[33] Rents increased most and fell least in the highland zone, on account not of landlord investment but of population pressure.[34]

If isolated examples of reduction and remission are meaningless, they do in context exemplify the role of the several parameters of depression. Even so it remains difficult to disentangle these elements from the purely personal, particularly the attitude of the large landowner. Some remission had been given in most counties by the early 1880s, and new tenants were commonly offered lower rents than their predecessors. Occasional remissions as high as 50 per cent are noted at this early date, in Perthshire and Oxfordshire, for example,[35] more commonly 10 or 20 per cent was offered. By the 1890s substantial reductions were commonplace—40 per cent on the South Downs, for example[36]—but there were still plenty of unlettable farms; on the other hand in the Plymouth district a remission of not more than 10 per cent was noted,[37] and on the Derby estates in Fylde and Bowland (Lancashire) rents rose by one-quarter between 1884 and 1904.[38]

The trend was, therefore, for reasons already discussed, for rents to fall further in the lowland than the highland zone, and perhaps more continuously. Even within the highland zone a similar differential appears: while rents fell about 16 per cent in Monmouthshire, they fell only 1 per cent in Cardiganshire.[39] 'Strong' land, in other words the heavier clays, was at a disadvantage; in the Carse of Gowrie 'strong' land rents were down by a half by the 1890s, but rents in general by only a quarter.[40] The value of some heavy land reached the point at which it was only half the cost of bringing it back into full production.[41] This differential also had a regional component: cold clay near urban areas in Yorkshire was fetching 36s (£1.80) an acre while similar land was fetching at best 10s (50p) in Essex.[42] Remoteness from the railway was another factor tending to depress rents.[43] Marginal hill country within the lowland zone was also unpopular. By the 1890s rents were down 40 per cent in the Blackdown Hills of the Devon-Somerset border, but only down 15 per cent at the most throughout North Devon,[44] and in the Cotswolds rents fell by 50 per cent, but in the Severn Vale by only 20 per cent.[45] This differential receives much less comment in Scotland and Wales, where elevated marginal land was commonly abandoned.[46]

Dairy districts were particularly well placed, no county, for instance, suffering less than Cheshire, where rents fell by 10–12 per cent.[47] In the dairying areas of Dorset rents dropped by 10–20 per cent, but in poor arable districts by 40–50 per cent.[48] Grazing localities were similarly favoured, rents on the Duke of Rutland's estate near Melton Mowbray, for example, falling less than those in most of Leicestershire.[49]

Generally arable land was less sought after than pastoral, but self-sown grass was almost worthless—2s 6d (12½p) per acre in areas where permanent grass fetched 25s (£1.25).[50] Large farms in general commanded lower rents per acre than small, a situation accounted for by the scarcity of tenants with enough capital to take large properties, and by the greater proportional value of house and buildings on small farms.[51]

Dulac provides a neat summary of the situation based upon the work of Pringle, an assistant commissioner to the second Royal Commission, in the East Midlands. It is best expressed in tabular form:[52]

| | Rent per hectare (francs) | | |
	1878–9	*1893*	*Per cent Reduction*
Almost wholly grass	117·90	80·10	31·9
Principally grass	103·20	69·50	32·5
Half grass, half arable	114·50	73·35	35·9
Principally arable	104·00	65·00	37·1
Good Soil	100·35	69·35	30·8
Medium Soil	91·35	57·25	38·4
Inferior Soil	85·00	48·35	43·6

Rent falls have been estimated by only a few writers. In 1907 Thompson[53] calculated that on an index of 1867–77 equalling 100, rents reached a peak of 106 in 1877–8 and a low point of 75 in 1901, for England and Wales; the problem of collecting rents must, however, also be recognised, Maxton estimating only a 90 per cent level of success in Scotland in the early 1890s. His estimate of the fall in rents for Scotland is just over 20 per cent between the late 1870s and mid-1890s.[54] Evidently England and Wales experienced a fall in rents rather less than the contemporaneous fall in prices but rather greater than the increase experienced in the 1850s, 1860s, and early 1870s. Clearly in some localities, for many individual landowners, rents fell more than prices; it is moreover apposite once more to question whether indices of prices truly reflect the necessary pattern of expenditure of either landowner or farmer at this time.

CAPITAL VALUES

Capital values fell more spectacularly, though rather less quickly, than rents. In Dorset, for example, rents fell by 30–50 per cent and values by 40–60 per cent;[55] and in Cumberland rents by 15–25 per cent and values by 30–35 per cent.[56] There was little enthusiasm among buyers—'potential purchasers were not readily convinced that land was really cheap'[57]— and sellers were reluctant with values so depressed. Only the really unfortunate sold land, one example of such a sale being the Bowers Welham estate in Yorkshire, where in the 1890s mortgage interest exceeded the rental of the 1870s.[58] On an estate in South Yorkshire Beastall noted a disinclination to buy land after 1872.[59] As Thompson has pointed out, the market almost withered away, many auctions proving abortive, and land changing hands at seemingly ridiculous prices.[60] The minimal prices may probably be ascribed to forced sales, through bankruptcy, for example, and specific examples may well be misleading. Peewit Island in Essex sold for £8,000 in 1875, and for £420 a decade later;[61] the Plush Manor estate in central Dorset was valued at £17,000–£18,000 in the bankruptcy of the Weymouth bankers Eliot, Pearce & Co in 1897, to which it contributed, but it had been bought for £28,000 in 1879 and had been improved to the extent of £12,600.[62]

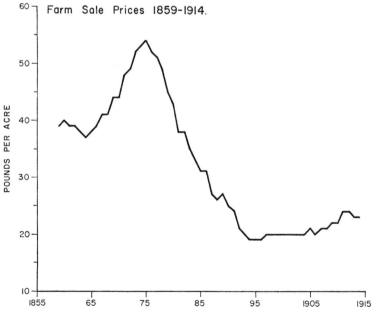

Fig 15 Farm sale prices (England and Wales) 1859–1914 (Ward, *Estates Gazette Centennial Supplement* [1958], 49)

The value of land sold in England and Wales fell from £54 per acre in the mid-1870s to £19 in the mid-1890s (Fig 15);[63] but, as has been pointed out, this diminution of 65 per cent probably exaggerates the real fall. As Lady Bracknell observed, land had become a liability rather than an asset,[64] and one wit suggested to the second Royal Commission that it should be bequeathed to enemies rather than friends.[65]

By the 1890s land commanded a purchase price of only 20–25 years rental—a reduced rental at that—where formerly 30–40 years was the norm.[66] Predictably values fell more in the south and east than the north and west: even dairy land lost half or more of its value in Wiltshire,[67] whereas for Selkirkshire 30 per cent is quoted,[68] and the figure of 50 per cent quoted by Garnett for Westmoreland seems improbably high for one of the least affected counties.[69] Rateable values are often a good index of local changes: the valuation of Northleach Union in the Cotswolds fell from £67,000 to £37,000, though Thornbury Union in the Severn valley was reduced only from £94,000 to £87,000.[70] By the late 1890s, however, demand and value had sharply revived for some hitherto almost worthless land now suitable for horticulture. Land near Wisbech changed hands at £100 to £150 per acre when formerly it would have been 'given away with a pound of tea'.[71] The revival was belated but speedy, land near Spalding being almost unsaleable as late as 1894, when the bulb industry was already well established.[72] Rents reacted to such prospects similarly, rising at Blairgowrie from 25s (£1.25) to £4 12s 0d (£4.60) per acre.[73] The effect of the depression, however, was to write off, at least in lowland Britain, the rise in rural land values characteristic of the third quarter of the century, the free agricultural markets of the last quarter of the century, in fact, invalidating commercial, and sentimental, assessments of the value of landed property made in exceptional and ephemeral circumstances.

THE TURNOVER OF TENANTS

Landlords were faced during the depression with a number of problems parallel to the fall of rents. The turnover of tenants increased; some farms could not at some periods be let at any price and the owner had to consider either becoming a farmer on his own account or allowing the land to become derelict. In general, and particularly as they took place, these phenomena have been given undue emphasis; they were the ephemera of the depression rather than developments of lasting import. But those who saw them took them very much to heart; and some, notably Pringle, an assistant commissioner in the 1890s, had the pen to do them almost melodramatic justice.[74] Derelict or neglected land was conspicuous, its extent easily exaggerated; it was a sharp change from the meticulous standards of mid-century prosperity.[75] Moreover it was not a

POSITIVELY OSTENTATIOUS.

Mr. Phunkstick (quite put out). "TALK ABOUT AGRICULTURAL DEPRESSION, INDEED! DON'T BELIEVE IN IT! NEVER SAW FENCES KEPT IN SUCH DISGUSTINGLY GOOD ORDER IN MY LIFE!"

Mr Punch always enjoyed making fun of timid sportsmen. The context (1894) is of rural dilapidation

matter of the misfortunes of an apparently affluent social minority, as with rent reductions, and did not, like them, invite a degree of disinterest and detachment in the social and political climate of late Victorian England.

The turnover of tenants appears to have increased generally, but the movement out of the highland zone to empty farms in the lowland zone created few vacancies in the former area, even where there were also many failures.[76] There is, however, little doubt that turnover was more rapid in the depressed areas. Commonly custom as to tenant right favoured the outgoing occupier, a stimulus to leave in the early years of depression, as also did the abandonment of leases and their replacement by annual agreements during the depression period. Such developments inconvenienced the landowner in several ways. Tenants had become hard to find in many localities, more or less regardless of rent, thus even unsatisfactory tenants were often retained, though they would have been evicted in normal circumstances.[77] Good farms were never hard to let at an appropriate rent, but many farms required wide advertisement, formerly an exceptional procedure. In 1894 a Cambridgeshire landowner advertised vacant farms in the *North British Agriculturist, Lancastrian Guardian, Fife Herald, Stamford Mercury, Midland Counties Herald, West Cumberland Times,* and *Scottish Farmer,* a fair indication of where he thought new tenants would be easiest to come by in difficult times.[78] Changes of tenancy also meant argument about, and payment of, compensation, and when bidders were scarce, the increased risk of acquiring an unsatisfactory tenant. Almost certainly it would also mean a lower rent.[79] It is thus no surprise that some landlords regarded changes of tenancy as a sphere in which they must act in person. In 1879 'Squire' Chaplin visited his Lincolnshire estates: 'When it comes to so serious a question as farms being given up it is a matter on which I must decide things for myself, and on which Burton [the agent] can hardly act for me. Besides which I could keep them when he couldn't'.[80]

The exact extent to which changes in tenancy increased is uncertain. The obvious, and comprehensive, source—advertisement in local newspapers—indicates a minimal increase in Cheshire, and greater increases in Dorset and Huntingdonshire,

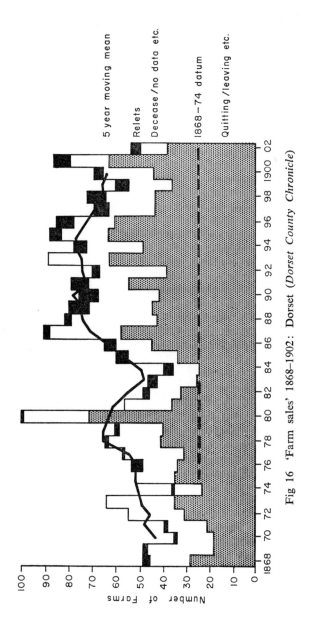

Fig 16 'Farm sales' 1868–1902: Dorset (*Dorset County Chronicle*)

the only counties which have been thus examined. These two latter counties were moderately and severely affected respectively, and the number of advertised sales of live and dead stock and farming equipment are given in Figs 16[81] and 17. Rew, the assistant commissioner who visited Dorset in the early 1890s, did not himself believe there had been an abnormal turnover of tenants,[82] a warning perhaps against the too ready acceptance of the views of expert outsiders on long-term trends in particular districts. A high turnover of tenants did not, however, necessarily imply numerous vacant farms, as was pointed out with respect to Northumberland, Lincolnshire, and the Severn Valley;[83] but the converse was invariably true. Nor did change of personnel, as in the

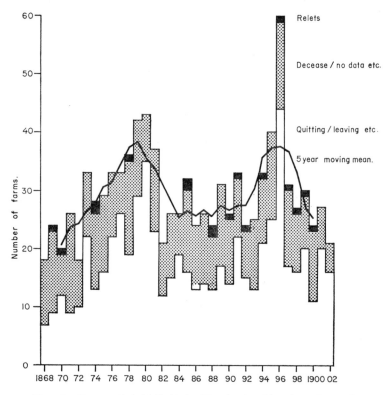

Fig 17   'Farm sales' 1868–1902: Huntingdonshire (*Peterborough Advertiser*)

Lothians,[84] necessarily imply a radical change of farming system.

Unlet land constituted a further problem. It appeared very early in the depression—in Essex in 1872, in south Warwick-shire by 1875[85]—but most extensively in the acute later phases. In Dorset, for example, the acreage advertised to let, an approximate index of this situation, was no more than a few hundred acres a year in the late 1860s, a maximum of 21,000 acres in 1880, and over 7,000 acres each year between 1875 and 1895.[86] There is a suggestion that the first phase of intense depression served to flush out the really weak and incompetent, as well as perhaps the shrewd and farsighted, and that there-after, if tenants were not necessarily more tenacious, replacements were more easily found. The figures quoted for Dorset are by no means exceptional, for the *Stamford Mercury* reputedly advertised 16,000 acres to let in one week,[87] but too much weight should not be placed on such figures, since notice of intention to quit and advertisement were sometimes nothing more than the thrust and parry in a campaign to obtain a lower rent.

More credence may well be given to some contemporary estimates, even so in round figures rather than exact terms. In the early 1880s about one-quarter of the land in Caxton Union in Huntingdonshire was reported to be unlet,[88] as was about one-eighth of the Oundle district in Northants.[89] These districts were in the worst affected area at this period. By comparison about 5 per cent of the Yeovil district in south Somerset was unlet, most of it heavy land and much of it unwanted because of the depredations of sheep rot.[90] The unlet farms between Newmarket and Brandon were by comparison light land farms suffering from an excess of game.[91] The Commissioner of HM Woods and Forests reported to the Royal Commission in 1893 that almost 4 per cent of his wide-spread estates were in hand.[92] Generally the lowland zone was most adversely affected—Essex, the east Midlands and central southern England in particular—but within this area some districts, like Norfolk and Lincolnshire,[93] escaped com-paratively lightly. There are also some surprising anomalies, such as grassland unlet in the Fens in 1880.[94]

Uncultivated derelict land was an extreme exemplification

TUESDAY NEXT.
CARTER'S and LONG LANE FARMS,
EAST HATLEY, Cambs.
ALL THE
Valuable Live and Dead Farming Stock
In use on a 400 acre occupation, comprising
9 Powerful CART HORSES, NAG COLT, BLACK COB, PONY,
COW, TWO STEERS, CALF, and about 200 Head of Poultry ;
DEAD STOCK
Comprises 4-horse-power Thrashing Machine with Drum, 8-coulter Drill, 5 Tumbrel Carts, 6 Iron Ploughs, 5 Sets of Iron Harrows, 4 Turnip Cutters, Harness for 8 Horses ; also
The Cropping of the above,
Comprising 20 STACKS of CORN with the Straw, 4 STACKS of HAY and CLOVER, 2 STACKS of STRAW, a large quantity of MANURE ;
And the whole of the
HOUSEHOLD FURNITURE
Comprising Cottage Pianoforte, several Feather Beds and Bedding, Dairy and Kitchen Utentls, and the usual Domestic Requisites,
TO BE SOLD BY AUCTION, BY
WM. WALLIS,
On TUESDAY next, October 19th, 1880, at Ten for Eleven o'clock in the Forenoon, commencing with the Furniture, on the premises of Mr. Charles Edwards, under a distress for Rent.

The Stacks will be allowed to stand upon the Land until the 25th day of March, 1881.

Catalogues may be had of the Auctioneer, 185, East Road, Cambridge, who will post them on application.

(East Hatley is situated about 2½ miles from Gamlingay Station, on the London and North Western Railway.)

A 'farm sale' advertisement 'under a distress for rent'—a common occurrence during the depression but always less common than 'quitting' or 'leaving his farm'. From the *Cambridge Chronicle* of 16 October 1880

of the problem of land-letting, a difficult and controversial issue, whose importance was often exaggerated. Pringle wrote of parts of Essex where 'whole farms and tracts of country have been abandoned and given up to nature'[95] but also commented that this was largely a reflection of the character of the soil; only a few miles away was well farmed land, none of it uncultivated.[96] There was abandoned land elsewhere, in the Chilterns and Cotswolds, for example, and marginal land recently brought into use in the highland zone was abandoned;[97] but even in severely affected areas it seems that less than 1 per cent of land became derelict, though locally the percentage might be higher.[98]

The real problem was, as it remains, one of definition; for every one of the few thousand abandoned acres at any one time there were many more of tumbledown grass, or even bare fallow, worth next to nothing and supporting only a few sheep and cattle during the summer. The general decline in the tidiness of farming—skimped cultivations, neglected weeds, overgrown hedges—further complicated the issue.[99] The bulk of unlettable land was not abandoned but became the responsibility of a generally reluctant owner for as long as he judged it impossible or unadvisable to let.

THE LANDLORD AS INNOVATOR

Many landowners, probably the majority, found farming on their own account unprofitable. The Duke of Bedford, for instance, recorded a loss of £23,116 as a farmer in the period 1879–96, in an admittedly very depressed area.[100] Even as skilful a farmer-landowner as Edward Strutt lost money when times were hardest—in 1892–3, for example.[101] Undoubtedly the fact that land was often 'in hand' because former tenants had left it in a foul condition, or because it was the poorest land, made things more difficult; one landowner summarised his role as 'a sort of residual legatee of the worst land on my estates'.[102] Nevertheless some landlords appear almost to have relished the task and opportunity. Strutt had 854 acres in hand in 1876 but 4,315 acres by 1896.[103] Only in a few years did he make a loss, and he laid the foundations of an enduringly successful group of enterprises. Lord Wantage farmed

F

13,000 acres in Berkshire in the mid-1890s and proved him-self a social and commercial as well as an economic innova-tor.[104] Economies of scale and management rather than a radical change of system epitomised his approach. Most land-lords were not of the calibre of Strutt or Wantage, but made do—and lost money—during those periods when tenants were unobtainable. When times were easier, as in the years around 1890 and later in the same decade, advertisements for the sale of stock and equipment on a landlord reletting his farms quickly appeared in the provincial press.[105]

The depression also provided the landowner with oppor-tunities for innovation, although he was less conspicuous in this role than the farmer. The development with which the landlord was most closely associated was the grassing down of arable land, the most characteristic and probably most sensible land-use change of the depression period. But grass-ing down was an expensive long-term investment, a gamble in a period of falling rents; unlike drainage it was not an improvement for which money could readily be borrowed. The Duke of Bedford found that between 1878 and 1889 grassing down cost anything from 29s (£1.45) to 200s (£10) per acre; one of the most cheaply grassed areas fetched only 15s (75p) an acre 14 years later, the rent having fallen 45 per cent, a dubiously satisfactory result. But what of the 64 acres grassed down at £10 per acre for which the rent fell from 27s 6d (£1.37) to 5s (25p) during the same period?[106] Lord Leconfield did rather better, grassing down at £12 10s 0d (£12.50) per acre, returning 4 per cent and lifting rents from 13s (65p) to 30s (£1.50).[107] Dukes and lesser lords could sur-vive such losses and raise the necessary capital. But how many small owners were in so favourable a position? Grassing down, however, was often a prerequisite for obtaining a tenant,[108] and possible losses had to be weighed against the cost of taking the property 'in hand'. Despite such problems it was a most characteristic way of assisting tenants, often associated with a better field water supply which was essential to any move towards livestock husbandry.[109]

A much smaller group of landlords appear as genuine inno-vators, a few almost as eccentrics. On the Peel estate in Bed-fordshire, for example, heated greenhouses were provided.[110]

Lord Wantage provides a more rational example as a pioneer of co-operatives, smallholdings, and even profit-sharing; he built roads, planted shelter-belts, built cottages and improved water supplies.[111] He made no fortune, but gained a lasting reputation and was at least able to carry on. A few land-owners were among the scientific pioneers, notably Elliott in Roxburghshire who, through several financial crises, evolved a system of stock feeding based on temporary grasses and a wide variety of crops.[112] However, it must be admitted that in the matter of innovation landlords missed rather than seized their opportunities, perhaps most notably in forestry.[113]

Finally the landlord had to accept and participate in some changes which were imposed from above, substantially because of the depression, and these were not always to his liking. The Agricultural Holdings Act of 1883 established tenant right on a legal basis and, unlike its precursor of 1875, did not allow the landlord to contract out; the Ground Game Act of 1880 gave new privileges to the tenant in an area closer to his everyday relationship with the landlord; and the establish-ment of county councils in 1888 challenged and changed the landowner's role as a rural legislator. In fact the owner appears more often as an acceptor than as an originator of all the changes characteristic of the depression; it is a perceptive view of the period which sees as one of its hallmarks the transfer of leadership from landowner to farmer in a variety of rural spheres.[114]

LANDLORD ECONOMIES

In the depression years many landlords were forced to economise. Not all landowners, not even all great landowners, had a sufficiently large non-agricultural income to enable them to persist in their accustomed way of life or to subsidise estate expenditure. For the most part, however, the periphery rather than the core of the country-house life-style was the subject of economy; and a few contemporaries later noted how easy it was to live through the depression without notic-ing it. 'It was possible to be born and come to maturity in the countryside of those last two decades of the century with-out ever having one's attention called to its existence, for, to

the uncritical eye, nothing could have presented a more speci-
ously prosperous appearance than the face of the Victorian
countryside in the splendid and imperial sunset of a reign.'[115]
The illusion was not only in the aristocratic mind, for in the
rural classic *Lark Rise to Candleford* Flora Thompson noted
of the early 1890s: 'Everybody in those days seemed to do
well on the land, except the farm labourer'.[116]

Characteristic areas of domestic economy were recreation,
education, and in the last resort the house itself. Shooting
was commonly let; it was sometimes worth almost as much as
the value of the land for farming.[117] Hunting was reduced:
the Duke of Beaufort, for example, cut hunting at Badminton
from 6 to 4 days a week, 'lent' part of his country, and took
subscriptions for the first time.[118] During the years 1889–92 the
historian G. G. Coulton taught at Sherborne, and in his autobiography half a century later he noted: 'The agricultural
depression . . . had changed greatly the attitude of many
families for whom, in earlier generations, Eton or Harrow or
Winchester had been instinctive. In Sherborne Schoolhouse,
therefore, were probably a score of boys whose fathers, or
even elder brothers, had been at great, dignified, and costly
schools'.[119] It is tempting to speculate whether the depression
played a part in securely establishing the position of the
second-rank public schools in late Victorian society.

Non-residence was usually a policy of last resort, but in
some areas it appears to have been quite common. Jefferies
commented: 'Old mansions that have never been let before
can now be hired for the season'.[120] Halèvy asserted: 'Landlords no longer lived in the country to make their money;
they visited the country to spend it'.[121] Some believed that non-
residence had particularly pernicious effects, since the kind of
affluent townsman who hired a country house for his family
set a bad social example, which some farmer's wives and
families were only too ready to ape, and the townsfolk's ignorance of agriculture made them unsympathetic neighbours.[122]
Thirty years later Robertson Scott blamed the rural housing
problem on the landowner who lived away from his
estate and was thus readier to neglect or economise on his
property.[123] Some landowners, however, found the experience
less disagreeable than they had expected: 'We have five farms

on our hands. We have hired for a trifling rent the Rectory in our parish which chanced to be vacant. We have broken up our establishment here, and we have a better balance at our bankers than we ever had in our lives before'.[124] Not everyone was so fortunate, for the country-house tenant was sometimes as reluctant to pay his rent as the hard-pressed farmer.[125]

Corporate landowners, and perhaps most small landowners, found it particularly hard to economise. Hospitals, colleges, and the Church were particularly affected.[126] The fellows of Downing College, Cambridge, admittedly never a rich society, had to forgo their dividend on at least one occasion.[127] The canons of Winchester, Salisbury, and Gloucester were placed on half stipend for a period in the early 1890s, and 'Winchester wondered for a time how to stay open'. Glebe-dependent incumbents might be even worse off; in some east Midland dioceses they lost three-quarters of their income.[128] In the University of Cambridge low professorial salaries, a consequence of depression, made it very difficult for some elderly professors to retire in the 1890s.[129]

Economies in estate expenditure raised more difficult and complex problems, some of which, as has been mentioned above, were of long-term significance. In the highland zone, where rents remained high, the economy issue was relatively unimportant; in the lowland zone the question was not only one of falling rents, but one compounded by the need to spend money to facilitate desirable changes in farming practice.[130] Livestock husbandry and dairy farming called for different buildings and a different range of equipment from arable high farming. Some landlords had shrewdly foreseen that this kind of situation was likely to arise; acting accordingly they spread necessary expenditure over a longer period, and thus avoided the worst of the depression. Others did not, or their estates were not readily adaptable to changed circumstances. Heavy losses on the Bedford estates appear to relate both to lack of foresight and to a physical environment inimical to changes in the system of farming.[131] Some landlords, the larger in particular and the Duke of Bedford among them, had non-agricultural incomes with which to support their rural properties; but at the other extreme an unfortunate group had not only to live off a shrinking rent income but to meet a burden of inherited debts and jointures.[132] There remained the large group whose gross income decreased, who had to make some economies, and who like everyone else regretted the fact that traditional standards and attitudes could no longer be maintained.

This variety of circumstances met with a number of responses, some of them seemingly contradictory. In Cambridgeshire, for example, McGregor noted a drop in reinvestment from about one-half to about one-fifth of gross income on one estate, but an increase from 7 to about 20 per cent on another.[133] Certain broad trends are, however, apparent: Perren noted a broad correlation between sustained expenditure and sustained rents, and a generally higher level of reinvestment in pastoral than arable districts extending back into the years prior to the depression.[134] On the other hand Thompson noted that heavy investment in mid-century often resulted in a burden of over-capitalisation during the depression.[135] Expenditure on drainage was usually high in the late 1870s and early 1880s while the problem was still seen in climatic terms and while this area of investment could be afforded,[136] but thereafter it diminished sharply in many, though not all, cases. Some reinvestments were more readily abandoned than others, such as purchase of land on the margins of the estate, and repairs and maintenance, surely a factor in deteriorating landlord-tenant relationships,[137] but there is some evidence that the percentage of gross income reinvested did not substantially change. Thompson estimated 27 per cent in the early 1870s and 22 per cent in the late 1880s;[138] but with falling rents the sum of money spent substantially diminished, and there is some evidence that costs of repairs and improvements fell rather less quickly than prices as a whole.[139] In the last resort the outlook and the fortune of the landowner remained paramount: Strutt's success reputedly reflected an aversion to expenditure other than on drainage, the Duke of Bedford was forced to subsidise his rural properties, and Lord Wantage combined investment and economy. It is quite possible that totally different approaches might have served equally well.

There was then no common landlord experience of the depression, no single satisfactory response. The effect of the depression was widely uncomfortable, but as has been pointed out, landowners unlike farmers were rarely forced to sell up, and only occasionally became non-resident. It is, however, an open question as to how far the experience of 30 or more unprofitable years, for rents rose but slowly in the aftermath of the depression, and of a deteriorating social and economic position made landowners the more ready to sell up in the period before and after World War I. It has been customary to regard the last quarter of the nineteenth century as the Indian summer of English landed society in its traditional form;[140] perhaps it was also the dawning of a new rural scene.

4

Farmers in the Depression: Finance, Migration and the Size of Farms

THE FARMER'S EXPERIENCE of the depression broadly paralleled that of the landowner in its principal feature—a falling income. Almost 90 per cent of farmers at this period were tenants,[1] and the existence of a community of interest between such farmers and their landlords was generally taken for granted: 'The landlord's interest is the tenant's interest, and vice versa', as one farmer witness put it to the Richmond Commission.[2] Discussion of the landlord's problems has necessarily revealed the main features of the tenant's position. These must be recalled at this point, and it must be remembered that although good landlord-tenant relations were usual, there was in the last resort an element of subservience and dependence. Sir Mathew Ridley did not hesitate to tell the Richmond Commission: 'If I had reasonable cause to suspect that a man was falling into bad habits [ie excessive drinking] I should use every personal influence I could with him, and if I could not succeed . . . I should terminate the tenancy.'[3]

THE FARMER'S FINANCIAL POSITION

The farmer lost, or thought he lost, money during the depression on account of adverse seasons and falling prices; profits like rents were smaller and harder to come by after the

92

mid-1870s than before. Nevertheless most farmers continued to make some kind of a living, and a few a very good one. A mass exodus of farmers characterised only a few very difficult localities. Diversity of experience in space and time was as typical of farming receipts as of rents; the most skilled and most fortunate farmers lost money even in the worst areas only in the toughest years, and others had their savings from better years. While there is some evidence that farmers were —and probably always had been—more prone to financial failure in the lowland zone than the highland zone,[4] the second Royal Commission found examples of both very profitable and very unprofitable farming within a few miles of one another in the lowlands during a very depressed period.[5] In other words, and, as has already been observed, personal ability counted for a great deal in the success or otherwise of the farmer, probably more so than with the landowner. Any model of the depression must take this fact into account. Moreover farming was an occupation much more easily entered or left than landowning, particularly during the depression, a factor further favouring diversity of experience and outlook.

Unfortunately the farmer's experience of the depression was not only more varied than the landowner's, but also much less well documented. Estate records were commonly adequately kept and preserved, but farm accounts were not. The majority of farmers seem to have kept no accounts other than their bank book, and an honest few admitted to chronic financial ignorance. 'Can you give me any idea of what profit you make on a cow in the course of the year? I have no idea . . .' was one exchange before the Richmond Commission.[6] The minority who kept accounts were probably unrepresentative, more than typically shrewd and energetic; but their accounts were not always satisfactory, let alone sophisticated. The problem was a real and not wholly soluble one; several Royal Commission witnesses were essentially advocates for the keeping of accounts,[7] and by 1894 the subject was part of Cambridge University's agriculture course.[8] But as Strutt, an innovator in this area, pointed out, problems remained, such as cost accounting for yarded cattle.[9]

The situation was thus one of widespread complaint, abundant indirect evidence, but very little direct financial evidence.

Of the small number of accounts examined by the second
Royal Commission, a few more show loss than profit,[10] but
the sample is not only small, some 40,000 acres, but unrepre-
sentatively biased towards the lowland zone and the bad years
of the 1890s. It would thus appear that a majority made at
least a paper profit, even if a small and uncertain one,
although, as has been pointed out, there is evidence that in
the lowland zone even the experts lost money in the worst
years. Against this kind of experience must be set falling food
prices, reduced or remitted rents, and, for the entrant to
farming, lower capital requirements.[11]

Loss of capital was the farmer's most basic experience of
the depression, and the most serious and substantial of his
losses. Moreover it was common knowledge that successful
and profitable farming required adequate capital, and that
many farmers began with too little.[12] In fact capital losses were
sometimes unrecognised until a farm changed hands, but they
often took place very quickly. Little believed that Wiltshire
farmers lost 40 per cent between 1877 and 1881, and an East
Midlands land agent went as high as 80 per cent for the
Nottinghamshire clays between 1875 and 1880.[13] Loss of
capital may, paradoxically, have kept tenants on their farms,
able to make a small living but unable to provide an
adequate capital sum for retirement or even debt repayments.
As one Cumberland farmer put it: 'More men can sit than
fly'.[14] Estimates of the reduction in occupiers' capital during
the depression have been as high as 50 per cent, comparing
Giffen's estimate of £677·5 million in 1875 with several of
about £360 million in the mid-1890s. Giffen's estimate is
probably too high, but that of Boreham, £479 million for
1874–8, omits unexhausted improvements;[15] between 30 and 40
per cent is perhaps a fair approximation. One element in this
loss was the falling value of money, but other issues were
involved; the farmer in difficulties often lived off his capital
as well as his income, to the detriment of his landlord's
and his successor's interests.[16] Not a few farms were deliberately run down by tenants who took them on for this purpose
as restrictive covenants were relaxed in order to find tenants.[17]
The Agricultural Holdings Act of 1883 partially remedied
this situation.

Farming on a reduced capital, treating capital as income, took a variety of forms. Certain inputs, such as feeding stuffs and fertilisers, were reduced or disappeared. 'He disposes of his stock to pay his debts and labourers; he gets into arrears with his rent; he signs bills and promissory notes; he seeks the assistance of dealers and moneylenders; and all the while he is letting down the condition of the land he farms.'[18] The presence of dealers' stock, already commented upon, is not invariably a sign of diminished capital, but there is no doubt that this phenomenon became more and more common during the depression. Farmers' equity diminished, while that of their variously secured creditors increased. An important element in this situation was a reluctance among farmers, particularly among their womenfolk, to accept a lower standard of living. There is a grain of truth as well as a comment on contemporary attitudes in the remark, 'When the farmer has to begin to work himself it is a bad job'.[19] But many contemporaries saw in such an outlook an important secondary cause of depression. Brodrick placed it alongside excessive borrowing and undercapitalisation,[20] and Jefferies acidly remarked: 'Has not some of the old spirit of earnest work and careful prudence gone with the advent of the piano and the oil painting?'[21] A high standard of living remained the hallmark of success: 'That a farmer can take his day's hunting and give his womenfolk a piano and a dogcart is surely one of the best proofs that he can make his intelligence and his capital pay', wrote Hall in 1913.[22] In such circumstances it is scarcely surprising that farm economy rather than farmhouse economy was much discussed and practised during the depression.

THE CHANGING FARMING POPULATION

Most but not all contemporary authorities refer to an increased turnover of tenants, in such different farming environments as Sussex and Northamptonshire, for example;[23] elsewhere it was denied—in parts of Yorkshire, and, less expectedly, Oxfordshire.[24] Intensity of depression and changing manpower and management were not, however, always spatially correlated, as Orr noted in Oxfordshire;[25] and what might be regarded as a rapid change in one district would be regarded as normal elsewhere, as with the risk of failure in good or bad times. In Berkshire, for example, tenancies usually lasted longer in the Vale of the White Horse than on the Downs.[26] It is thus no surprise to find contradictory views of the situation expressed in a single area: 'I did not gather that farms have changed hands to any abnormal extent', was Rew's comment in Dorset in the 1890s.[27] Local opinion disagreed and is supported by the advertisement columns of local newspapers (Figs 16 and 17). In Dorset this material suggests that on average twenty-five 'farm sales' a year came about through a tenant quitting or leaving in the period 1868–74; between 1875 and 1881 forty-one sales of this kind occurred each year, between 1882 and 1888 thirty-eight, between 1889 and 1895 fifty, and between 1896 and 1902 forty-seven. In Huntingdonshire the increase was even sharper, but rather less sustained by comparison with Dorset. The Bedfordshire pattern resembles that of Huntingdonshire, but in Cheshire turnover increased only slightly, by little more than 10 per cent in 1875–81 compared with 1868–74. Rather surprisingly, however, Westmorland evidence indicates an elevation of turnover which was early and sustained, such as would not be expected in the relatively lightly affected highland zone. The evidence is not strictly comparable, relating to farms to let rather than 'farm sales', but, as has already been pointed out, is nevertheless suggestive. The number of farms so advertised was twice as numerous each year in the period 1879–81 as in 1868–71, and remained high in the early 1890s. This rich vein of evidence has, however, been no more than prospected; it awaits exploitation.[28]

The figures quoted above suggest a slower turnover of farms than some contemporary comments imply; these latter may be unreliable or extremely localised, but the newspaper advertisement evidence does not cover the occasional moonlight departure and the more frequent transfers within a single family. One witness before the second Royal Commission claimed that every farm but one in the Ampthill district had changed hands in little more than a decade,[29] and another from Staffordshire estimated the normal occupancy in the relatively depressed south of the county at about 20 years through the whole period from the mid-1850s.[30] Newspaper evidence cannot refute these absolutes, though it can effectively compare depression and pre-depression experience.

Probably the majority of those who left did so because they were unable to continue; a minority, early in the depression in particular, retired to live on their capital. One witness to the Richmond Commission, a land agent, estimated that as many as one-third of the tenants in the depressed upper Thames valley could have thus retired had they so wished.[31] There were, however, numerous disincentives in either case. Leaving a farm, or changing farms, necessarily involved even a good farmer in some loss, even in such counties as Yorkshire where customary tenant-right favoured the outgoer.[32] Landlords were often forbearing and mortgagees disliked foreclosure when land values were so low. Other creditors were inhibited by the law of distress, but from the late 1870s moneylenders were seizing stock from farms in Northumberland.[33] Generally the large farmer could leave more easily than the small, the tenant than the owner-occupier.

In either case giving up farming meant leaving the family home, and most farmers had no other profession to turn to. A number emigrated,[34] and a number moved up and down the 'farming ladder', amassing holdings of thousands of acres or becoming labourers or bailiffs. One witness noted that some took seaside boarding houses,[35] others compromised and took part-time jobs;[36] but the majority of those who left the land have, from the scholar's viewpoint, sunk without trace. In the latter part of the depression evidence appears that a number of men who wished to leave were in no position to do so: 'Hundreds of men cannot break, they have not enough to break on' was a Norfolk viewpoint.[37] Sir John Lawes commented to the second Royal Commission: 'Look at the value of a man's capital; his wheat and barley are worth hardly anything; his capital is gone, and that is why he hangs on, because if he goes out it is lost'.[38]

Those who entered farming during the depression were a varied group—migrants from the north and west, local farmers' sons, in the face of paternal discouragement, able labourers and shepherds, urban businessmen and industrialists. Probably the majority came from the locality or nearby; in south Staffordshire they were observed to come mainly

from the north of the county, and from Cheshire and Derbyshire;[39] and Cornish landowners claimed that they were drawn
primarily from local farming families.[40] In Northumberland
shepherds took farms.[41] One Scottish assistant to the second
Royal Commission provides detailed information on this
matter, although with respect to a district, Nithsdale, not
severely depressed: 172 of its 245 farms had had new tenants
since 1879, and ninety of these were farmers, fifty-three
bankers, merchants and the like, nineteen farm workers, three
agricultural students, and seven proprietors.[42]

The general preference was for small and accessible farms.
The newcomers were neither uniformly skilful or successful; in
the North Riding, although largely small farmers' sons, they
were described as a poor lot.[43] Their capital resources were
also variable, although one advantage of taking up farming
at this date, and an important element in the recovery from
depression, was that a shrewd man could enter a low rented
farm on the best of terms and with a minimum of capital.[44]
A few intelligent farmers seem to have foreseen this possibility
and returned to farming with the real value of their capital
enhanced a decade later—in East Yorkshire, for example.[45]
The general impact of new men on farming defies even the
modest generalisation possible with respect to Scots and
Westcountry migrants discussed later in this chapter. Some
thought they were more industrious and practical than their
over-cultural and over-leisured predecessors; others regretted
an influx of 'non-practical' men.[46] Some were so inept, incompetent or unlucky as to survive only a few years,[47] but a
number brought in new skills and attitudes, new resources
with which to build up large holdings or develop new and
profitable systems.

MIGRATION FROM THE HIGHLAND ZONE

Among the movements of farmers, that from the highland to
the lowland zone has received the most attention; it is one
of the few aspects of the depression to have been the subject
of a scholarly monograph.[48] Its interest verges on the romantic
in its elements of success from failure, triumph in adversity.
The movement itself, however, was not new. 'Go east for a

farm, go west for a wife' is an old Scottish proverb; there is evidence of a long-standing drift of farmers from north and west to south and east,[49] and of traditional connections between the two in the movement and purchase of livestock for fattening. As late as the 1870s Welsh-speaking drovers attended Bodiam Fair in Sussex.[50] What was new was the acceleration of this movement in the early 1880s, when opportunities presented by depression in Essex, in particular, and the lowland zone, in general, were taken up.

The best known and most numerous members of this stream were Scots, from Ayrshire and neighbouring counties, and Westcountrymen; their most usual destination was Essex, Suffolk or Hertfordshire. In fact the movement was more widespread, although the streams already mentioned were the most numerous and persistent. Lanarkshire men set up dairies for Glasgow in Kinross,[51] Welsh graziers moved into the Midlands, and a few Scots took up farms in Wales and the Isle of Man.[52] In some areas movement was in series, Devonshire men, for example, replacing Somerset farmers who had moved to the eastern counties. Movement within the lowland zone is evidenced by advertisement and application—a farm advertised in west Dorset, for instance, drew a response from as far afield as Warwickshire and Kesteven in 1891.[53] But characteristically and pre-eminently movement was of small farmers and/or their families from over-populated and high-rented pastoral districts to larger arable farms in low-rented areas. These people had no other skills than farming and a limited chance of using even these to their best advantage in their home areas; the depression was an exceptional opportunity for the ambitious among them to climb up the 'farming ladder'. The number involved is uncertain, probably no more than a handful in most cases—for example, there were reputedly twenty Scottish dairymen in Suffolk in 1894[54]—and there is no evidence that such migration was more than a desirable thinning out of congested areas.

Only a few localities witnessed invasions. Smith thought that by 1930 almost a quarter of the farmers in Essex might be immigrants or their descendants, and that the Welsh were comparably numerous in the Rugby district. Between 1880 and 1900, the depression period, 170 farmers from the highland zone took up farms in Essex—about two-fifths from Scotland, almost as many Westcountrymen, and the remainder largely from the northern counties in the 1890s. The figure given by Pringle is probably higher and predominantly Scottish;[55] he wrote as the movement occurred, but it was not the prime objective of his study, and he may have been misled by the fact that the Scots were a most conspicuously alien group.

On the whole the migrants succeeded. Failures are mentioned, but persistently only in the East Midlands and the Andover district.[56] Some went home from other localities, probably but not certainly a sign of failure, though in one case it was attributed to the lack of cider![57] The basis of success was twofold—hard work and skill. The incomers worked hard, and economised on labour by changing rotations and using their family. In Essex, for example, the Scottish seven-course reduced labour by one-third compared to the traditional Norfolk four-course.[58] The facts that they were not too proud to work in the fields and were willing, at least in the short run, to accept a lower standard of living than their predecessors and neighbours were likewise important. Some were endowed with capital, others bought land at such low prices as £20 per acre inclusive of the cost of its restoration to cultivation;[59] most were not so well placed but were attracted by massive rent reductions—from 35s (£1.75) to 4s or 5s (20–25p) per acre on the Duchy of Cornwall Berkshire estates, for example.[60] Berkshire had its Westcountry migrants, perhaps attracted by the common landlord. A few migrants, like the Somerset and Dorset farmers in Sussex,[61] even accepted the now unpopular leases.

The other basis of success was the blending of old and new knowledge, of adapting skills learned in one environment to new surroundings. Thus many Scots specialised in potatoes in Hertfordshire and Oxfordshire,[62] and even more in dairying, bringing and continuing to buy cattle from Ayrshire.[63] Westcountrymen likewise favoured dairying and rearing on grass, and perhaps retained home links: Devon cattle were fattened in Sussex, for example.[64] Arable farming by no means disappeared; the best known Essex Scot, Primrose McConnell, an agriculture graduate of Edinburgh University, grew cereals on his heavy land at Ongar, but not seeing 'how cheap wheat was to pay the expenses of dear fallow' used temporary grass, and insisted upon a high standard of cultivation for weed control.[65] Some Scots also gained a reputation for the lavish use of artificial fertilisers.[66] Not all immigrants achieved or aspired to McConnell's high standards. Bare fallows returned, some farmers were 'robbers', and heavy land always remained a problem.[67] In a few areas immigrants closely followed local practice, Barnstaple men in arable Suffolk specialising in barley,[68] and Welsh graziers conforming in the Midlands. The migrants were, perhaps naturally, criticised as much for their successes as for their failures, and particularly for labour economies or personal frugality. One acid Essex witness observed to the second Royal Commission: 'You cannot starve a Scotchman'.[69]

Such immigrants were a blessing to hard-pressed landlords, who advertised for them,[70] employed agents,[71] and kept their eyes open when visiting Scotland in person.[72] In a few areas in Wales landlords replaced the evicted natives with Scots, a particularly unpopular move.[73] No doubt personal communications also played a part among friends and relations. Farming in a new environment proved not only profitable but even pleasurable. There is surprise and elation in a comment recorded by Smith: 'Eh man, this is the first year we have had no rent to pay, and the first year we have had money to pay rent with'. There is also evidence that a milder climate and a new social life were not unimportant; the latter may have appeared limited and impoverished to local farmers, but to the migrants it was a change for the better. But above all at least the majority of these farmers were successful, and a number were pioneers and innovators, occupying and making a good living from land otherwise half-farmed or not farmed at all, and soon emulated by their neighbours.

THE SIZE OF FARMS

The question of the size of farms also received considerable attention during the depression, not as a cause, nor because there were major structural changes, but through a genuine and at times puzzled curiosity as to whether there were significant relationships between farm size and some features of the

G

depression, and because a policy of closer land settlement, of smallholdings in particular, was vociferously advocated as a solution to rural social as well as economic problems. Such different figures as Ernle and Jefferies shared an admiration for the French peasantry;[74] and eleven chapters out of twenty-five in Pratt's *The Transition in Agriculture* (1906) are concerned with peasant holdings, market gardening, and co-operation. The best known of all land reform slogans—'Three Acres and a Cow'—was coined by Jesse Collings in 1885, reflecting a view that the solutions to Ireland's rural problem might have some application in Britain. Two Acts of Parliament, in 1892 and more effectively in 1907, and some private initiative did establish many smallholdings—nearly 13,000 by 1914[75]—but too many were never more than marginal and had become a sufficient problem by 1968 to warrant investigation by a Royal Commission.

The social context and the diversity of experience account for the fact that most commentators have found this topic a particularly hard one for assessment; the second Royal Commission found it so, and such experts as Clapham and Venn echo this view.[76] It is particularly hard to decide whether large or small farms better withstood the depression, and to discover significant trends in farm size. Demand for farms of various sizes and the relationship between size and rent are less contentious issues.

The small farm and the large—the small pastoral and the large arable, in particular—were better able to withstand the depression than the middling. Worst off was the group 'too high in the social scale to use their own labour, too low to possess more than a little capital'[77]—in fact a large, possibly majority, group. By comparison the small man employed no paid labour and could readily turn to quasi-subsistence and a low standard of living;[78] alternatively items such as fruit and poultry,[79] which he was particularly well placed to produce, enjoyed a favourable market, especially if he was near a town. The larger farmer could survive by adopting the most extensive and least intensive practice, or if he had adequate capital on which to retire.[80] This last possibility probably misled a few contemporary commentators in assessing merits of size in farms. In fact the large farmer was, at least in the long run, probably better placed than the small man with limited savings and reserves, too high a rent, and too little capital. The small owner-occupier with a mortgage was particularly badly placed—as in Axholme, for example[81]—even allowing for tolerant mortgagees. In general the small farmer who survived did so by accepting very low standards of living and farming practice, as was commonly observed by the Welsh Land Commission and in such small-farmer counties as Cumberland.[82] Although large and small farms were to be found in most counties—Jessopp found plenty of small farmers to write about in Norfolk—the small might be regarded as more typical of the highland zone, the large of the lowland. These latter when farmed extensively—ranched, in fact— were particularly conspicuous in the landscape, another element tending to generate misunderstanding and exaggeration.

In general the number of small farms increased, as much spontaneously in prosperous horticultural districts as through government action; and very large properties also became more numerous as enterprising individuals took on more and more farms and acres. The effect on average size was thus limited; and it was further confused by the fact that the very large units commonly comprised several farms, and were recorded as such.[83] Subdivision and aggregation were thus parallel and contemporary processes; while the Ecclesiastical Commissioners divided farms and similar developments occurred privately, as in Leicestershire,[84] consolidation was going on in the same county and the East Riding.[85] On the whole the former was applauded, the latter regretted, although several of its exponents had begun in a very small way. A holding of 70 acres, for instance, at East Hendred (Berkshire) grew with a loan of £200, into 3,000 acres.[86]

The demand for farms during the depression was for the small rather than the large, despite the marginal economic advantage of the latter.[87] The small farmer occupied the bottom rung of the 'farming ladder', but even so he was usually undercapitalised.[88] In areas such as Yorkshire tenant-right favoured movement to smaller farms.[89] By comparison tenants with the capital and the technical and managerial skills to manage more than a few hundred acres were never abundant; in the depression they almost vanished, despite the reduced capital requirement. Some politicians scarcely regretted the fact, and a few such holdings were successfully broken up into smallholdings. Rew near Dorchester was thus, and remuneratively, developed after being unlet for several years, some areas changing hands at twice their former value, and the rateable value increasing.[90] In good times in Weardale miners sought smallholdings as a security against bad times.[91] Elsewhere there were less successful schemes; small properties were often to be found in the wrong area and environment, such important matters as marketing were neglected, and microcosms of unprofitable arable farms were created.

Finally the rent of the large farm was relatively less, since it had to be substantially reduced to attract a tenant.[92] House and buildings formed a larger proportion of the value of small farms and, together with a higher level of demand, were the reason for relatively higher rents. In this sense small farms were more vulnerable to depression, several commentators noting that their rents fell more quickly into arrears;[93] in practice this disadvantage was substantially compensated for by a move towards subsistence, and perhaps by a greater willingness and capacity for hard work and belt tightening.

The size of farms was a contemporary issue, and changing patterns of farm size were a contemporary phenomenon. But their relationship to the depression was generally marginal. The attention given to the topic reflects not the context of depression but the context of aroused and vocal political concern for the character of rural society and its economic base, often, however, seen through spectacles which had already taken an over-rosy view of the continental European situation.

5

Farmers in the Depression: The Practice of Farming

ECONOMIES

THE FARMER, LIKE the landlord, had to find ways of meeting his reduced circumstances. The most obvious of these, although not necessarily the most effective, was to economise. 'Retrenchment not development had to be the order of the day; yet it was not these who pulled through, but rather those with sufficient resources and/or ability to attempt producing new commodities by improved methods.'[1] In this comment Astor and Rowntree are overplaying their hand, for economy could work. Was not aversion to expenditure one of Strutt's talents?[2]

The most obvious area of farming economy was labour, an expensive item whose price, having risen sharply, seemed less inclined than most prices to move downwards during the depression.[3] Rural depopulation facilitated labour economies by limiting rural unemployment, thus making this policy socially acceptable. In some cases it was a rational and very quick reaction to unduly meticulous standards in the high farming decades, but even where economy went further its short-term effects on yields were slight. Hedges were neglected, the number of cultivations reduced, and weeding was skimped, even in wet years when it was most needed. 'Only what is absolutely necessary is done' was a Lincolnshire comment.[4] The problem existed on grass as well as on arable farms, but

105

was less readily noticeable on the former.[5] In Haddington-shire (East Lothian) another long-term consequence was noted, the decay of such trades as ditching and drystone dyke build-ing, dispensed with in hard times.[6] Where the farmer could afford it, machines could replace men.

As to domestic economy, there is the occasional mention of less hunting,[7] but otherwise very little except in the case of small farmers. These led, as already noted, notoriously frugal lives, the more so in hard times and in the high-rented highland zone. Very often they had no paid labour on which to economise. Their success as tenants in such areas as East Anglia was reputedly related to the acceptance of a low stand-ard of living as well as to new methods.[8] Even in intensively and highly commercially farmed areas the small farmer in general had a hard time. Augustus Jessopp asked the wife of a high-rented tenant of 50 acres in his Norfolk parish how they managed: 'Why you see, sir, the corn about pays the landlord and such, and then we reckon to live, and there's seven of us and we all help, I don't know how we do, but we keep going!'[9] The tenacity of the small man in avoiding the descent to labourer status or in taking a first upward step on the 'farming ladder' is to be admired, but it often contained a harsh and grim aspect for his family, and sometimes a persistent one.

All farmers depended to a considerable extent on their creditors' forbearance if they were to survive hard times. The landlord was the most important of this group, and privileged by the law of distress; nevertheless dealers, bankers, and merchants also played a part, if perhaps one which diminished as the depression continued. The general reluctance of most such creditors to press their claims to the limit, however, evidences shrewdness as much as charity; it was better to hold on and keep a debtor going in the hope of better times than to force liquidation or bankruptcy and probably receive only part payment. Owner-occupiers, often expensively mortgaged, were worse off than tenants in this respect; mortgagees were much less willing than landowners to reduce the level of payment, but the collapse of land values made many if not all mortgagees reluctant to foreclose.[10] In a few cases, however, landlords bought out embarrassed owner-occupiers, at their own request, and accepted them as tenants.[11]

GRASSLAND FARMING

In the broadest terms, however, the characteristic economy in farming practice during the depression was a simple one: the cultivated acreage diminished, while permanent grassland increased. When the collection of agricultural statistics annually began in 1866, there were 17·5 million cultivated (tillage and temporary grass) acres in Britain, at a maximum in 1872 there were over 18·4 million acres, and in the late 1890s usually a little under 16 million. Permanent grass covered 11·1 million acres in 1866, 14·4 million by 1880, and 16·7 million by 1900. Rural Britain in the decade 1866–75 had 45 per cent tillage, 11 per cent temporary grass and 44 per cent permanent grass; but for 1896–1905 comparable percentages were 32, 12, and 56.[12] More striking changes are evident for particular items: the wheat acreage was over 3 million from 1866 to 1875, but after 1893 it was rarely over 2 million until World War II, and occasionally less than $1\frac{1}{2}$ million; and there were nearly 28 million sheep in 1866–70, but 2 million fewer by 1896–1900. In fact this apparently simple response to falling cereal prices contains a number of components, the aggregate of numerous individual solutions to the problem of making farming pay. 'The question . . . is one which every farmer can answer for himself. Scarcely two farms or the systems upon them are alike . . . he may, in fact, deviate in a hundred ways from the beaten track by high farming or high feeding, and in this way command success', observed a farming handbook in 1892.[13]

There were numerous alternatives to unprofitable traditional high farming, many calling for no evidently radical change, except in the use of labour such as characterised a shift into dairying or horticulture. These alternatives could range from a modest slackening of 'high farming', often by adopting new and longer rotations originating in Scotland,[14] through a return to older systems of minimum outlay and slower turnover,[15] to the virtual ranching of a few sheep or cattle on 'tumbledown' summer pasture made up mainly of weeds.[16] Not only the intrinsic merits of such systems had to be considered but also the skill, inclination and capital resources of the farmer, price levels and future prospects, and, pre-eminently, rents. The 'lowest' farming could only coexist with the lowest rents. There remained the perennial element of chance and uncertainty.

Throughout the depression a very common change was to substitute barley or more commonly oats for the wheat crop.[17] These made lesser demands on soil fertility than wheat, were more suitable as livestock feeds and less of a gamble in adverse seasons. Their prices seemed more stable than wheat prices; with barley there was always the chance of a good malting sample, and with oats a secure and remunerative market in the towns. In fact the barley acreage shrank very little during the depression, and occasionally the average price, and undoubtedly more often the actual price, exceeded that of wheat. The acreage of oats increased by about 20 per cent between the late 1860s and the late 1890s, and it proved so remunerative and so adaptable in new rotations that in 1913 Hall felt constrained to comment on oat sickness in such areas as the Blackmore Vale.[18] It was wheat, the dearest cereal for human consumption, able to stand the cost of importation and suited only to a limited area of Britain, which bore the brunt of the depression. The marginal areas for wheat cultivation were most affected: Scotland's wheat acreage diminished by almost 70 per cent between 1866 and 1895, and Cornwall's by almost

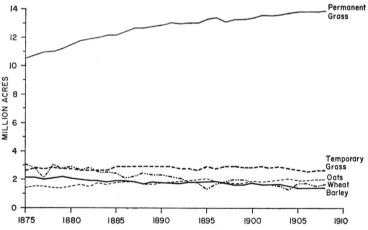

Fig 18   Acreage under cereal crops and grass (England) 1875–1908 (Besse, 352–3, from official statistics)

65 per cent between 1872 and 1895,[19] while in England and Wales as a whole the diminution was little over half between 1866 and 1895. This latter year was in fact the nadir of British wheat farming, followed by some expansion of acreage and higher prices (Fig 18).

Grassing down, the most obvious alternative to cereal growing, had begun well before the onset of the depression, which merely served to accelerate and extensify the process. It was probably at its peak during the first phase of intense depression, but the grassland acreage reached a maximum some years after the depression during World War I. As a technique, and a problem, grassing down generated a vast and contentious literature, notably in the *Journal of the Royal Agricultural Society*,[20] but, as has been pointed out, it was an expensive and uncertainly profitable long-term investment.[21] Many farmers and landowners preferred, therefore, to make use of temporary or rotation grasses and clovers while hard times prevailed, but often these were left down for much more than the intended 2–3 years, becoming permanent *de facto* if not *de jure.* Neither the seed mixtures used nor the methods employed favoured their establishment as permanent pasture; moreover too little fertiliser and too much grazing was often their fate in the circumstances of the depression.[22] In the moist and mild western counties temporary grasses could develop into useful permanent pasture; but in the dry east and the cool north this was rarely the case, especially on heavy soils. Poor grasslands capable of carrying very few stock, let alone fattening them, were the result.[23] This is not to deny either expertise in grassing down or in using extended rotations: Lord Leicester on light land in Norfolk established 6–8 year leys primarily for sheep or mowing, emphasising the need for good quality seeds and the avoidance of overstocking, with a break of cole-seed, oats, turnips, and barley to avoid sheep sickness,[24] and R. H. Elliott and others saw the value of grass and developed systems of ley farming at Clifton Park, for example.[25] Feed crops such as tares played their part in such diversification when the seasons allowed, and Scottish migrants to the south-east often found a place for the potato if they were close to an urban market.[26] Catch-cropping was one of the few intensifications characteristic of the depression; but since such crops were often autumn-sown for spring feed, they had no impact on the annual crop returns.[27] One other root crop of increasing importance was the mangold, because of its usefulness for winter milk production, 259,000 acres in 1866 having become 400,000 by the turn of the century. By comparison turnips and swedes, integral to arable high farming, had shrunk from over 2 million acres to about $1\frac{3}{4}$ million at the turn of the century. As ever, the best land offered the best chances; in the Chilterns Coppock noted that grassing down characterised the heavy clays of the vale, but a wider range of diversification better land in the uplands.[28]

The extent of grassing down is in some respects uncertain. Distinctions between permanent and temporary grass, rough grazing, and even fallow were, for reasons already discussed, difficult and inexact. Rough grazing only enters the crop returns, as 'mountain and heath', in 1892. Moreover the early crop returns, of the period when grassing down was well under way, are not wholly reliable. Coppock suggests an under-estimation of arable in the early 1870s of more than 2 million acres. The important feature of grassing down is its continuity, from before to well after the depression, and its geographical extent; it also stands out as one element in the depression which was well known and well understood at the time.[29] The quality of its end product is a matter of considerable import-ance but almost complete uncertainty; Pringle estimated that some two-thirds of that in Essex was 'tumbledown', full of docks and thistles and worth no more than a few shillings an acre. Scottish immigrants had set the farmers of this district an example of the possibilities of ley farming as an alternative to fallow in weed control, but Pringle claimed to see little real ley farming, and some 'bush'.[30] Essex was an extremely de-pressed county and a difficult environment for the establish-ment of pasture, so it is perhaps not unreasonable to surmise that throughout Britain at least half the increased grassland acreage was reasonably productive, though rarely first class.

New grass thus characterised not only the areas where it would grow well but those where almost no alternative (un-profitable cereals excepted) was to be found. Likewise bad years for the arable farmer meant more grass; in 1879 Sutton's laid down more than 10,000 acres of heavy land for their owners and farmers.[31] In better times cereals made their come-back. If some traditional high farming areas, such as the Lothians,[32] remained loyal to high farming, others moved strongly to grass. In Axholme, for example, the acreage increased by 20 per cent between 1887 and 1891.[33] Grass became an asset to the farmer in tactical manoeuvres with the land-lord; the threat to break up grassland was sometimes used to obtain a more favourable agreement.[34]

The reasons for grassing down were several, and the trend was already well established by the time cereal prices collapsed. Grassland economised on labour and concentrated on the more remunerative livestock, though in lesser numbers than on intensive arable farms. Milk production might be based on grassing down; and in some cases it was necessitated by the quest for new tenants[35] or the control of such arable diseases as 'finger and toe'.[36] At the time the saving of labour was considered the most important aspect of grassing down, though its extent varied; it must also be recalled that the switch to grass took place within a much wider context of rural de-population. However, some experts saw little spatial correlation between the two.[37] The Duke of Bedford reckoned that every 200 acres grassed down represented five labourers;[38] the Board of Agriculture thought in terms of even greater economies, ie one labourer to every 25–35 acres;[39] in Aberdeenshire three labourers to 100 acres was suggested;[40] and in Dorset only one and a boy.[41] Essex Scots commonly reckoned to halve their labour, but they commonly made great use of family labour.[42] Another labour-cost estimate reckoned the national average at 25s (£1.25), grazing at 10s (50p) to 18s (90p) per acre per annum.[43] In one or two counties the position was reputedly reversed, a labour shortage inducing grassing down in Dumfriesshire and Cheshire, for example.[44]

The stall-fed bullock and the folded sheep went the way of the farm labourer who looked after them. Summer grass-land fattening nicely matched farming economies and changing public taste, which came to prefer lighter and younger joints of meat;[45] thus while cattle numbers increased from just over 5 million in 1866–70 to over 6½ million in 1896–1900, those over 2 years old (other than in milk) scarcely increased in number, while those under 2 years old increased from 1¾ million to almost 2¾ million. Dairy cattle (in milk or calf) increased from just over 2 million to over 2½ million; as winter milk commanded a premium, the mangold alone among traditional root crops increased in importance, although some farmers preferred green crops for this purpose.[46] Sheep numbers declined during the depression, in part because of disease, but as Coppock has pointed out the figures conceal a substantial geographical redistribution away from the lowland zone towards the highland zone.[47] This reflected the demise of the arable flock and its replacement, at much lower intensities, by grassland sheep, or in some areas, such as Norfolk, by dairy cattle.[48] Thus Cheviot and Blackface sheep appeared on Salisbury Plain, reputedly reducing out-goings by four-fifths;[49] and the Dorset Horn for early lamb production was introduced to the Vale of Aylesbury.[50] A parallel development and economy was to buy cheap 'cast for age' ewes from hill farms which would thrive for at least a year or two on even poor lowland pastures.[51] Nevertheless an important consequence of the grassing down of the lowland zone was to disrupt the established and balanced relationship between upland breeder and lowland feeder, and thus prices and markets.[52]

Some problems remained, though some possibilities were neglected. Silage was probably the most important of the latter, a wave of enthusiasm in the 1880s quickly petering out. By 1912 not one of fifty-seven silos constructed a generation or so earlier in Westmorland was still in use.[53] Leases and the tenant-right question inhibited farmers in some areas of Scotland;[54] and they claimed that they were too poor to move out of arable into pastoral farming in areas such as the Vale of the White Horse.[55] It was not an improvement for which the landlord could easily borrow money,[56] and it might also necessitate investment in water supply.[57] The economic climate of the depression scarcely favoured long-term investment and grassing down was certainly in this category; the environmental problem in the dry eastern counties was exaggerated, but it existed and was not easily overcome. On the other hand basic slag, introduced in the mid-1880s, transformed the cold clay grasslands of the northern counties, a development pioneered by one of the great experimental farms of the period— Cockle Park, Northumberland.[58] Whereas 4,500 tons were used in 1887, one firm sold 6,500 tons in North Wales alone in 1895, an indication of the rapidity of its acceptance.[59]

The move away from arable into grassland farming covered a wide range of practices and possibilities. The general tendency was to lighter and lower farming, made possible by lower rents, and a return to a minimum outlay system of farming which had prevailed before high farming was developed. Less capital was required but it was turned over more quickly; certainly no less skill was called for. In many respects the pace of farming had speeded up, with more catch crops, and fat stock slaughtered at a younger age. The pre-eminence of live-stock over grain, perhaps a reality before the onset of depression, came to be accepted even in the context of cereal farming; 'My grain now all walks to market', said one Cumberland farmer.[60] Flexibility and foresight were as ever the basis of successful and profitable farming, even in the face of uncertain and ambiguous professional advice. It was possible in Essex in the early 1890s for 'low pressure' farming to return more than 10 per cent.[61]

DAIRY FARMING

The increasing importance of dairy farming, like the extension of grassland farming, can be traced back for some years before the depression, and continued beyond its end. The building of the railways, the disease and hygiene problem in urban dairies (culminating in the cattle plague of 1865–6),[62] and the increasing urban population and its rising standard of living, all made likely the expansion of dairy farming to supply fresh milk to the urban market, alongside or in place of traditional cheese and butter making. Depression facilitated this development: cheap land and empty farms became available,[63] in some instances near the cities; new and profitable farming systems to replace arable high farming were sought; and new men from districts with a dairying tradition moved into hitherto arable farms.[64] Supplying the cities with fresh milk almost ideally served these purposes; so perishable a commodity was practically invulnerable to overseas competition, and the railways could get it to the towns in good condition. Of all farm prices, that of fresh milk, especially of winter milk, fell least during the depression.[65] Moreover milk could be produced in a number of ways – on the new grasslands, or within a variety of arable systems.

A crude indication of the increased importance of dairying appears in the agricultural statistics in the increasing number of 'cows and heifers in milk or in calf'—about 1·7 million in 1866–70, over 2·1 million by 1896–1900—but this is almost certainly to underestimate the expansion of dairying for the urban market. Cheese and butter making were in decline and milk yields were improving. The railways witness very sharply to the increasing flow of milk to the towns: the amount carried by the Midland Railway, linking dairying counties such as Derbyshire to several urban markets, increased sixfold between 1872 and 1880,[66] and from $5\frac{1}{2}$ million gallons in 1881 to $8\frac{1}{2}$ million in 1888.[67] The GWR—'the milky way'—doubled its milk traffic between 1892 and 1910, and the LNWR's milk traffic grew by half between 1892 and 1904.[68] As Hall noted, access to the railway determined whether fresh milk or cheese was produced;[69] but by the turn of the century few areas outside the highland zone were more than a few miles from at least a branch line. This expansion took place from a relatively high base level, though one geared to manufacturing; as early as the late 1860s milk production was worth almost as much as wheat or beef and veal, at some £34 million a year,[70] though rarely given as much attention in debate and discussion by either landowners or farmers. Paradoxically milk was and remained scarce in rural areas; when W. C. Little held a meeting for labourers at Broad Clyst, Devon, 'a woman complained that she could not buy a ha'porth of milk'.[71]

The rise of urban markets, with their higher prices, was one factor in the decline of cheese and butter making. Why make butter and cheese when the milk required was worth nearly twice as much fresh as manufactured?[72] Moreover butter and cheese were imported in increasing quantities, notably after marine refrigeration was perfected in the early 1880s;[73] prices fell, certainly less sharply than for cereals, but more so than for fresh milk.[74] The late 1870s proved particularly trying for British cheese producers, farmhouse or factory; imports flooded in from North America, home consumption slightly diminished, perhaps because of industrial depression, and adverse seasons meant a poor supply of low quality milk.[75] In Dorset, for example, the yield of milk fell by a quarter, and production of cheese by one half in such years.[76] The depression was acute; a few witnesses before the Richmond Commission claimed that dairymen were worse off than cereal growers, and in a few areas dairy farms were given up.[77]

Perhaps this should also be regarded as a contributory factor to miscomprehension of the depression, for cheese prices recovered very sharply in the early 1880s;[78] nevertheless the last decades of the nineteenth century saw a steady if unspectacular erosion of the British dairy manufacturer's position. Butter imports, for example, doubled from 1·5 to 3 million cwt between 1886 and 1896, but consumption increased by only one-third between 1880 and 1911–1913;[79] as early as 1876 more than 1 million lb of margarine was imported.[80] If butter and cheese prices fell less than cereal prices, so did production costs. Cheese and butter making required skilled and expensive labour, and few farmers' wives and daughters were still ready to take their part in dairy work. Wages fell relatively little, and rents were less prone to fall in dairying than arable districts—in a few cases they moved upwards when land passed to dairying.[81] New labour-saving plant, like the separator, presented some possibilities to the cheese and butter maker, and purchased feeding stuff certainly became cheaper; but good labour remained the prime consideration, expensive but as yet indispensable.[82]

Dairying for urban markets was more than a change of methods and markets in established dairying districts near railways. It also embraced the development of dairying in primarily arable districts such as Essex and Wiltshire. In these areas this development was almost always associated with cheap land, and occasionally with very large-scale undertakings; S. W. Farmer, probably the largest of these, aggregated 14,000 formerly arable acres for this purpose around Pewsey.[83] On the technical side dairying ranged from extensive summer milk production on 'tumbledown' grass through virtual zero-grazing[84] to sophisticated, at times experimental, arable systems associating dairy production from roots, green crops, or grain with cereal growing, and aiming at lucrative winter markets. Probably the best known arable producer was Strutt in Essex, who went as far as developing his own retail outlets.[85] This was an important matter, and many major concerns such as Wilts United Dairies (now part of Unigate) had their beginnings at this time.[86] However, there is relatively little evidence of direct farmer participation in milk retailing on a large scale at this date. Strutt was also a pioneer of the Friesian, initially for crossing with the still pre-eminent Shorthorn;[87] and in the far south-west the Guernsey-Shorthorn cross was important.[88] A key role in many such developments was played by immigrants from the highland zone; many were from dairying districts, like Ayrshire and Somerset, and brought with them skill and even livestock while retaining contacts and purchasing young stock in their home area.[89] Moreover they, and their families, were not too proud to work in the dairy, an important matter in a labour-intensive industry.

It is scarcely possible to find an area of Britain where dairy farming was not on the increase during this period. Heavy land in Essex and the Weald, arable north Lancashire, sheep land in Norfolk, and grazing land in Leicestershire witnessed similar developments.[90] Specialised markets developed in some areas —the Reading biscuit-makers for parts of the Chilterns, for example.[91] Prejudice also existed in some areas: it was encountered by McConnell, best known of the Scots immigrants in Essex;[92] and in a few areas, such as Glamorgan, dairying developed less than might have been expected.[93] Standards were not universally high, despite the efforts of such societies as the Bath and West and the emphasis given to dairying in vigorously expanding rural technical education.[94] But if dairy beasts were poor specimens in some localities—Holderness, for example[95]—and advocates of bull-licensing votes in the wilderness,[96] increasing yields towards the end of the century[97] provide evidence that progress in scientific methods in breeding and management were not wholly unknown. Thus Kuhn demonstrated the distinction between the maintenance and production ration in 1887.[98] The pig remained the poor relation in the dairy, even though one contemporary shrewdly recognised his role as 'the gentleman who pays the rent';[99] supplies of skim milk did not completely dry up and were in a few localities the basis of specialised production, such as poultry at Heathfield, Sussex.[100]

(*above*) Loading vegetables for market c 1900. Location uncertain, and there is no evidence that this is land turned over to horticulture during the depression. Note the labour- (and animal-) intensive character of the scene, the non-working farmer, and the cumbersome returnable baskets (see p 120); (*below*) the landscape of depression—Bothenhampton, Dorset, c 1900. Overgrown hedges, ivy-clad house, patched and dilapidated thatch (see p 127)

Page 118

Haymaking on the Wantage estate, Lockinge, Berks, 1906. A labour-intensive activity in which women as well as men participate in the most arduous tasks. Note also the large number of horses used (see p 87)

The move into dairying was widespread, but it was not devoid of problems. The foremost among these was labour, which has already been discussed. If machinery could only displace some labour, other technical developments were a particular blessing to the dairyman: barbed wire, an American development of the 1870s, was one example.[101] Transport was a second problem—to the railway station, and more seriously to the city. The farmer was very much at the mercy of the railway company and disputes were common. Predictably many of these related to charges, although some were halved during this period; but perhaps more often they concerned conditions of carriage—such crucial matters as delays, consignments left standing for hours in the sun, and damaged churns.[102] Fraudulent urban buyers who adulterated or watered milk were another problem.[103] The seasons also raised difficulties. The poor summers of the late 1870s affected cheese makers in particular, and there were even, exceptionally, a few instances of liver fluke in dairy cattle.[104] In the 1890s it was dry summers, reducing dairy output by almost one-third in Derbyshire in 1893.[105] On many formerly arable farms buildings were unsuitable for dairying, and many landlords were unable or unwilling to provide replacements; financial difficulties also deterred some farmers from changing over.[106] Finally milk production was socially and technically unattractive to many farmers brought up on the idea that corn was king. To them farming was growing crops, preferably wheat, and fattening stock. By comparison dairying was monotonous, restrictive, and a step down the social ladder. Such factors were important enough to the farmer, pre-eminent to his wife and daughter. They cannot be reduced to statistics, but their reality is attested in contemporary literature to the extent that they cannot be ignored.[107]

No contemporary doubted that the dairy farmer fared as well as any of his peers, and better than most, during the depression, especially if he moved in at the bottom. As Venn has pointed out, this was not merely a matter of relative immunity from overseas competition but of the fact that dairy farming in general involves a quicker turnover of capital than almost any other branch of farming, a sure recipe for success in hard times.[108] Strutt lost money only in really bad years,

F

and his profit exceeded £1 an acre between 1888 and 1891.[109]
Witnesses before the second Royal Commission cited returns
of 12½ per cent from grassland dairying by Essex Scots, and
6 per cent from arable dairying in the same county.[110] No
meagre living by any standards, it was unfortunately not, as
Chaplin pointed out, a universally applicable panacea.[111]

HORTICULTURE

'The only form of agriculture which has exhibited any sign
of progress in recent years' was the appraisal of the fruit
industry made by a committee of the Board of Agriculture in
1905,[112] fulfilling Caird's prediction of 1878.[113] Exaggeration,
even a little complacency, no doubt, but there is abundant
evidence that horticulture as a whole had expanded its acreage,
and sustained its profitability, more than any other branch of
farming during the depression. Between 1873 and 1904 the
orchard acreage increased from almost 150,000 acres to almost
250,000 acres, and the small fruit acreage estimated at 37,000
acres in 1881 was recorded as 70,000 when first officially collected in 1897.[114]

Horticulture shared most of the advantages of dairy farming. Its home market was growing in size and affluence and
becoming increasingly accessible by the railways, and overseas competition was at a disadvantage, although less completely precluded than for fresh milk. Some commentators
argued that foreign suppliers did no more than whet and
develop the British consumers' appetites for the home producer
to satisfy.[115] Domestic horticulture was no new phenomenon,
no creation of the depression, save in a few localities; as with
dairying, it appears almost certain that some expansion was
inevitable. The depression served to accelerate this growth and
to shape its spatial dimensions.

Established districts certainly increased in importance during this period, although there are occasional references to
foreign competition, to adverse seasons, and even to land
being turned over to other uses.[116] (Bad seasons may well have
been an important reason why diversification into fruit and
vegetables was not characteristic of the early depression
period.)[117] Evesham and Sandy, to cite but two examples, were

localities where the horticultural acreage increased, and in the former fruit farming attained pre-eminence in the local agricultural economy.[118] In a few western counties, however, the horticultural acreage grew relatively slightly—the old established orchards of Herefordshire and Devonshire, for example —although a switch from cider production to eating apples was noted in the latter county.[119] The explanation almost certainly lies in the paucity of low-rented arable land in the pastoral western counties; it was in this economic and social environment that the most striking opportunities and innovations were to be found, and such environments were mainly in lowland Britain.

A number of now well established horticultural localities began in this way—cheap land, an enterprising individual and his imitators. The Worthing glasshouse industry, bulbs around Spalding, fruit around Wisbech, celery in the Isle of Axholme, are in this category,[120] though favoured by other advantages of soil, climate, and urban proximity. In almost every case railway transport rates were very important; the example of the usually impoverished Great Eastern Railway in offering competitive rates and reliable service helped many areas in East Anglia, and the results are evident in the growth of Stratford market, which doubled its fruit and vegetable trade between 1888 and 1898.[121] Cheap land helped initiate horticultural enterprise: around Spalding, for instance, land fetched £65 per acre in 1876 and £23 per acre in 1894.[122] Eventually this trend reversed, and by the late 1890s land near Wisbech was fetching £100 to £150 per acre.[123] Even on cheap land horticulture tended to be capital as well as labour intensive, fruit being reckoned to require £15 to £20 per acre in the early eighties,[124] and the element of risk was high.

There were problems; horticultural holdings were not licences to print money. The required technical and commercial skills were rather different from those of farming proper; so much so that the tendency of officialdom and opinion not to regard horticulture as a branch of farming, a possible area of agriculture diversification, is at times quite marked.[125] Like dairying, horticulture was a step down the social ladder, and at least one farmer confided to an assistant commissioner that he was unwilling to take this step because it would

necessitate working alongside his labourers.[126] Tenant-right
remained a problem in this area of long-term tenant investment; ideal customary solutions were localised, like the
'Evesham Custom', where the outgoing tenant nominated
his successor and received payment from him.[127] The Market
Gardeners Compensation Act of 1895 rather deterred landowners from letting land for fruit cultivation,[128] and not surprisingly owner-occupancy was regarded as ideal. There were
also environmental constraints. Horticulture was not restricted
to light land in southern and eastern England, for most fruit
trees do better on heavier soils and thus suited the kind of land
most readily abandoned by arable farmers. But the range of
opportunities was limited in the cooler and moister north,
where the only spectacular developments of this date were in
rhubarb forcing in the West Riding[129] and soft fruit cultivation
in Perthshire and Lanarkshire.[130] Chaplin's assertion applied
even more to fruit and vegetables than to dairying—only
favoured environments, and vigorous and skilful entrepreneurs
could succeed.

Politically the development of horticulture was favourably
regarded; noisy pressure groups approved of closer rural settlement, smaller farms, a more accessible 'farming ladder'.
Superficially at least horticulture fitted the bill, and smallholdings legislation from 1892 onwards favoured the trend,
and had established more than 12,000 enterprises by 1914.[131]
But appearances are misleading; many advocates of smallholdings looked rather to the French polycultural, quasi-subsistence, peasant model rather than to market gardens. Many
horticultural enterprises needed skills and capital not possessed
by the labourer, and many of the new smallholdings were in
unsuitable localities.[132] Contemporary evidence suggests that
legislation did little for horticulture, and that small farmers and
migrants from the towns, supported by urban businessmen,
were more important than farm labourers in this context.[133]

Other intensive, and hitherto neglected, farming systems
increased in importance at this time. Many migrant Scots
specialised in potatoes around urban centres;[134] and poultry
production, as has been mentioned, became the speciality of
such areas as Heathfield (Sussex), its methods and its profitability much and contentiously discussed.[135] In other areas

such universal, but hitherto almost always peripheral, activities increased in importance; the limited impact of the depression in Devon was ascribed to the attention given to poultry, eggs, butter and flowers. 'There is care taken with little things that you hardly find elsewhere'[136] was one comment. A few eccentrics advocated and made—or more probably lost—money from dovecots and rabbit warrens;[137] beekeeping became more widespread, comparable in its role and its possibilities to poultry farming, but even more vulnerable to the vagaries of the British climate. Who could make money from his hives in the cheerless summers of the 1870s? But in 1892 Graham observed: 'An old woman at Luffen Hall in Hertfordshire told me that she made £60 last year out of her bees. The small tenant farmers in the neighbourhood calculated, they said, to obtain the rent from the same source—say from £15 to £30'.[138] Forestry was the major possibility to be substantially neglected.[139]

Horticulture enjoyed hard earned, literally backbreaking, success rather than an easy triumph. There were failures through ignorance and lack of skill.[140] Some farmers advocated a kind of emulation of horticultural methods in farming as a whole—more intensive and quicker cropping[141]—but in practice to do this without incurring heavy profit-absorbing expenditure on labour and fertiliser was difficult. Equally remarkable is the fact that despite the prescient advocacy, by men of experience early in the depression, of the view that perishable products had a particularly bright future, many contemporary discussions on diversification say little on horticulture.[142] The ideal of traditional arable-livestock high farming died hard.

THE PERSISTENCE OF OLD METHODS

The fact remains that many farmers changed their methods relatively little, and wheat, a crop commonly claimed to be unprofitable, still occupied over $1\frac{1}{2}$ million acres at the end of the depression. The continuance and intensity of the depression was, at least in part, a reflection of this reluctance to change, of slowness in understanding what was happening on the part of farmers and landowners, of a hope that things would right themselves in time. It is scarcely surprising that in these circumstances the cereal acreage increased when and where the depression eased. In Brodrick's words, cereals were the 'besetting temptation of English agriculture'.[143] But in fact the persistence of grain growing contained a rational as well as an irrational, an informed as well as an ignorant, element.

Undoubtedly many farmers carried on growing cereals because skill, inclination, equipment and labour force favoured this activity. Moreover many of the economically more rational alternatives were socially degrading. In other cases financial weakness and even restrictive tenancy agreements kept farmers going in a system where capital expenditure could easily be evaded and 'hand to mouth' survival prolonged. There was also room for manoeuvre within cereal husbandry, though to an extent that was sometimes disputed. Barley and oats were readily substituted for wheat, and held their place in farming much better than wheat during the depression; at least one livestock dealer managed to integrate his activities into the essentially arable Norfolk four-course, though this was surely exceptional.[144] Straw always fetched a good price, and most farmers needed some straw; several contemporary writers make this point and many farmers geared their arable farming to this end.[145] Many farmers also claimed that their land was not suited to anything other than cereal cultivation; right or wrong this was nevertheless their assessment of their situation, on which they acted. Little's brother, a farmer near Wisbech, told the Richmond Commission: 'I do not know anything that we in our part of the country can cultivate instead of wheat at a profit'.[146] This same locality came to support a varied and profitable horticulture, an ironic indication of the fallibility of even the 'expert'.

Many farmers came to grow cereals not for the market but for their own livestock, preferring to make their farming system more self-contained despite the low price of purchased feeding stuffs. Grain grown for stock feed required less attention, and less investment, than that destined for the market; even if it was unprofitable, it was less conspicuously so. In general, yields increased very little during this period, the later 1890s perhaps excepted; the 10 year moving mean of cereal yields was often as high in the 1850s and 1860s as in the 1880s and early 1890s.[147] Despite a contraction of the cereal acreage on to the most suitable land, and the increased use of artificial fertiliser, a less intensive system, lower levels of stocking and less careful cultivation and weed control had direct effects.

A number of grain growers claimed that with lower rents cereal cultivation remained profitable. Channing, a member of the second Royal Commission who thought that the majority of his colleagues underestimated the severity of the situation, nevertheless exemplified a number of profitable traditional systems.[148] Hutcheson found wheat growing a satisfactory business even in Scotland in 1899 at a price of 26s per quarter;[149] in 1891 his Essex compatriot McConnell made a similar observation with the price at 30s per quarter.[150] There is no doubt that the capable individual could always make a living. Others pursued less orthodox systems. Prout's continuous corn growing on arable land was still profitable in the early 1890s,[151] and Strutt grew cereals on his Essex property after the winter roots, which were the basis of his dairy farming.[152] Some of those who assembled large holdings at low rents used them for cereal production: Baylis at Wyfield, Berkshire, used his primarily for barley production, for example.[153] But the adventurous and the capable were always a minority. Certainly more typical was the situation described by Coleman on the Yorkshire Wolds in the early 1880s. 'A radical alteration of system appears necessary, yet I could not find that much had been done by way of experiment.'[154] Most of those who continued as cereal growers did so because they were unable—or thought they were unable—or unwilling to break with known, established, and acceptable if presently unremunerative systems, or even to experiment within the arable context.

6

Labourers and Legislators

THE LANDLORD AND the farmer were cast in leading roles in the drama of depression; the labourer and the legislator made up the supporting cast. The labourers, numerically by far the largest part of the agricultural interest,[1] largely escaped the unpleasant consequences of depression. During the last quarter of the nineteenth century their money wages held up much better than agricultural prices. Real wages rose sharply,[2] and there were increasingly attractive and accessible opportunities for better paid employment outside farming. It was a depression for capitalists rather than wage-earners.[3] As far as possible the legislators avoided the basic issues of agricultural depression, preferring rather to talk, or to legislate, on peripheral issues.

THE LABOURER

Almost everyone agreed that the labourer was less adversely affected by the depression than his masters, but a simple optimism as to his fortunes is misplaced. The farm worker remained one of the worst paid of workers: in the 1870s, according to one authority, they 'did not live in the proper sense of the word, they merely didn't die'.[4] Exaggeration perhaps, but a more sober and scholarly assessment suggests that as late as this century many were underfed[5]—witness the standards required by the army.[6] Moreover during the depression there were no old-age pensions, few alternatives to the dreaded workhouse, and almost no effective agricultural trades

unions. Housing was often poor, and was a major area of
landlord economy during the depression.[7] There is also some,
though uncertain, evidence that relations between farmers and
workers, never particularly good, deteriorated even further
during this period.[8]

When these things have been said, the fact remains that the
agricultural labourer's financial position improved markedly
during the last quarter of the nineteenth century. At least some
labourers were able to save enough to rent or even buy farms.[9]
The sharp wage increases gained in the early 1870s, in part
the result of an ephemeral wave of rural unionism associated
particularly with Joseph Arch, were largely maintained through
a period of falling prices.[10] Moreover the labourer, unlike the
farmer and landowner, was much more nearly 'buying the
index', food being his major item of expenditure. Between
1875 and 1899 food prices fell by about 35 per cent, although
perhaps more markedly in urban than rural areas.[11] Generalisation about wages, and about working and living conditions,
is more difficult, but a cautious overview suggests that in
England and Wales the farm workers' average weekly wage
reached 13s (65p) in 1873 and 13s 8d (68½p) by 1878. There-
after wages fell slightly to be below 13s during the late 1880s,
but by 1898 they had returned to the 1878 level (Fig 19).

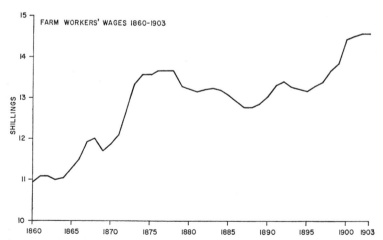

Fig 19 Farm workers' wages (England and Wales—sample of sixty-nine
farms) 1860–1903 (Besse, 347, from official statistics)

After 1900 these is some evidence that, though money wages rose, purchasing power diminished, a possible factor in the increase in emigration during the first decade of the twentieth century.[12] Regional and even personal variation in wage levels and wage changes was considerable: comparing 1870–71 with 1890–91 the Hertfordshire labourer moved from 10s 9d–11s 3d to 12s–15s (54–56p to 60–75p); the unfortunate Dorset labourer from 8s 6d–11s 6d to 10s–12s (43–58p to 50–60p); and the Durham labourer from 15s–17s to 17s 6d–18s (75–85p to 88–90p).[13] Predictably the labourer was better paid in mining, manufacturing, and urban districts than in predominantly rural and agricultural localities, but in these former areas he was generally less well paid than industrial workers. The farmers, it goes almost without saying, complained that high and recently increased wages were a cause of depression;[14] but these wages were paid and efforts to drive down wages as a solution to farmers' problems were few, even though wages generally displaced rent as the farmer's largest outgoing.[15]

Wages were maintained for several reasons, in the last resort because even in hard times the farmer needed his labour force and had to pay for it in competition with an increasing number of other potential employers. These latter set the lower limit below which the farm labourer's wage could not fall. In 1883 Thomas Hardy added another dimension to this apparently anomalous situation of high wages in hard times: 'The result (of Arch's efforts) has been an addition of three shillings a week to the eight or nine shillings the labourer used to receive. Such an increase in times of agricultural depression shows that he "must have been greatly wronged" in more prosperous times'.[16] Wages were high pre-eminently in relation to the appallingly low wages which supported the agricultural prosperity of mid-century. There were other factors involved. It seems likely that public opinion would have reacted strongly against any attempt to drive away depression by driving down wages, an expedient applied only to family labour.[17]

The obvious and widely applied alternative was to dispense with labour. 'Labour is the dearest article and the one soonest dispensed with.'[18] 'The rents that tenants do pay is paid by not providing labour'[19]—thus Lord Macclesfield's agent reduced the wage bill on an estate in the south Midlands from £1,256 in 1881 to £1,022 in 1888 without reducing wages.[20] The labour bill on R. W. Foll's Chalgrave Manor Farm (Bedfordshire) was £987 in 1876, £648 in 1896.[21] Not surprisingly there was rural unemployment, particularly in arable districts and seasonally. Evans quotes one comment, relating to the early years of this century: 'I was brought up in Earl Soham and there were about fifty of us young chaps in that area without work after harvest'.[22] It was labour economy which led to an unkempt and dilapidated landscape. Grassing down set out to economise on labour, but at least it retained regular and skilled labour. Diversification into horticulture or dairying demanded as much or more labour than arable farming. In some instances machinery could replace manpower, notably the binder from the 1880s,[23] but mechanisation was as often a means of solving the problem of a scarcity of labour as a cause of rural unemployment, a change from early decades of the century.[24] Threshing machines—even standing crops—were broken up and burned not by rioting labourers but by despairing farmers.[25] Alternative employment in the towns and elsewhere drew workers out of agriculture and kept up wages through a variety of circumstances during the depression.

There were more than a million farm workers in Great Britain in 1871, but fewer than 700,000 by 1901, a change which provides an essential backdrop to the depression rather than one arising from it. In retrospect the development appears as inevitable and desirable, and though rural depopulation was often talked and written about during this period, it was rarely regarded as a fundamental threat to the national well-being, as it was in France. A number of factors favoured the exodus of farmworkers and their families: transport was more readily available, and accessible, as the railway network was extended; the bicycle was perfected;[26] and teachers and many country clergy encouraged the labourer to use such opportunities to better himself.[27] Compulsory and effective rural education was unpopular with farmers not only because it had to be paid for but because it ultimately deprived the land of its best labourers, giving them ideas inappropriate to their position. Hence one farmer from Kent commented, and many of his peers would have echoed; I would have them taught all that is necessary to fit them for what I call the highest place that they can attain to on a farm'.[28]

In a few areas, and according to some authorities, population trends and the condition of agriculture were closely correlated. Roxby and Ashby claimed that the arable districts were most affected, and that the more difficult areas within them lost more of their population—west Huntingdonshire compared with Suffolk, for example. The increased rural population of horticultural districts was also noted.[29] Elsewhere correlations with industry were found: in the Bromyard district of Herefordshire, for example, it was noted that the supply of farm labour was linked with the fortunes of the Welsh mines.[30] Druce believed there was a positive correlation between falling population and low wages.[31] Others noted that rural depopulation had begun in good times, and denied that significant relationships with the state of farming could be demonstrated, emphasising that the phenomenon was merely one of the circumstances, a fortunate one at that, in which the depression was set.[32] Rural depopulation both involved and alleviated rural misery and rural heartbreak; there seems little doubt that depression in a setting of stable or even increasing rural population would have engendered very much more distress. By the end of the century there is evidence of a real scarcity of farm workers, notably in dairying,[33] in some districts, such as the Severn Vale,[34] even though elsewhere there was some unemployment.[35] However, the evidence suggests that the depression never generated more than ephemeral or localised rural unemployment except among some classes of casual workers. Wet seasons meant that men were laid off in some cases, but often extra work later in the year compensated for that.[36]

The migration of rural labour no doubt depended on age and ability. Not one of the thirty-one London policemen drawn from Jessopp's Norfolk parish in 30 years was a Sherlock Holmes—the stage policeman of melodrama and farce is an evident rustic—but nor were they village idiots.[37] (A fortunate few labourers used their rural skills, like East Anglians in Burton maltings, and horsemen in many towns.)[38] Thus complaints as to the quality of labour left to them were added to the farmers' complaints about cost and price.[39] In retrospect these were scarcely justified, for output per worker increased by almost one-fifth between 1867–9 and 1894–1903, although this is rather less than the increase in productivity in mining and manufacturing during this period.[40] The great gains in labour productivity in agriculture were as yet 50 years away.

Shedding surplus labour, as has been noted, made for an untidy and unkempt countryside[41] but it also made good economic sense; poor and extravagant use of labour (because it was cheap) was a fundamental weakness of mid-century high farming in the lowland one, and a shortcoming commented upon by the frugal Essex Scots.[42] Labour was not only traditionally cheap and inefficient, but also, and not unimportant in this context, underfed. A better diet certainly increased labour productivity during the depression,[43] which witnessed a wiser use of labour as its cost became a proportionately more important outgoing and as it became a better bargain. Labour costs were, on average, 36 per cent of net production in 1875–81, and they had reached 55 per cent by 1889–93.[44] Moreover the long-standing north-south differential in agricultural wages and farm workers' productivity started to disappear.[45]

To say that the labourer benefited from the depression is to give undue emphasis to one factor among the many which led to the amelioration of his situation. It is true to say, however, that relatively speaking he came through this period with much less stress and strain than his masters. Perhaps personal relationships had worsened; perhaps the countryside had become a dull and unattractive place in which to live, although there is an abundance of conflicting evidence on this point;[46] perhaps the period 1900–1914 is too easily viewed as a glorious Indian summer; but farm workers' wages had shrunk much less than prices, unemployment was relatively uncommon, and opportunity for advancement outside—even inside—farming was considerable.

THE LEGISLATOR

Until very late in the depression the legislator generally preferred to ignore its most basic feature. He was prepared to talk about the depression and to appoint Royal Commissions to investigate it, and he was prepared to legislate on a number of marginal problems, but he was not prepared to consider reimposing substantial protective duties. In any event the agricultural interest itself remained divided and uncertain as to the likely effectiveness of this traditional solution.[47] Some members always believed that it would work, and, with Newdegate, the last chairman of the Protection Society of the 1840s, still an MP, the matter was raised again in parliament as early as 1881[48] The origins of the ideas of Imperial Preference which materialised early in the twentieth century have also been ascribed to the early years of depression.[49] The evidence suggests, however, that many who thought that protection would put things right were aware that it was politically unacceptable, or perhaps even immoral. 'We do not ask the legislature to make the food of the nation dearer' observed the Abingdon Guardians almost apologetically in 1881.[50]

Early in the depression the widely held and not unreasonable view that adverse seasons were a major consideration encouraged a 'wait and see' attitude rather than any kind of legislative solution; only a minority actively advocated protection.[51] By the 1890s, however, the agricultural interest was more often, though not invariably, a protectionist lobby.[52] The focus of attention had shifted to the heart of the matter— prices. Strutt told the second Royal Commission: 'I want better prices, that is the only thing that will make things right with us'.[53] 'Fair trade' was a more acceptable public posture than protectionism, and it was under the even more respectable euphemism of 'Tariff Reform' that protection returned, at a modest level, to the cereal grower in 1902.[54] Veterinary legislation had given the livestock rearer some protection from imported cattle from 1892 onwards; its origins were almost certainly sanitary, its continuance was probably protectionist, its impact was rather limited, and if it favoured one group of farmers, it penalised another.[55] A high level of protection remained in the distant future, but as the depression progressed, more and more farmers and landowners became convinced that there was no other effective remedy.

Parliament preferred to think otherwise. First it must investigate—the role of Royal Commissions led by the Duke of Richmond and Gordon from 1879 to 1882 and by G. J. Shaw-

Lefevre from 1893 to 1895. Other major enquiries touched on the depression—the Welsh Land Commission in the mid-1890s, and the Royal Commission on Labour about the same time. There were also a number of committees on more technical issues: the Transatlantic cattle trade was considered in 1890, the sale of corn from 1890 to 1894, the decline of the agricultural population in 1906, and the fruit industry in 1905, to mention four very important examples.[56] The Royal Commissions, Richmond's especially, have often been accused of bias in their membership and in the way they called and questioned witnesses,[57] a perennial failing of such government-appointed investigations. Everett, a member of the Shaw-Lefevre Commission, after agreeing with a witness that the total disappearance of rent would be a calamity, began his next question with the observation 'I am rather inclined to think you differ there from some gentlemen who sit around this table',[58] an attitude generally supported by a reading of the evidence. In the case of each Commission, however, a key role was played by a small group—the chairmen; Kingscote and Chaplin, the Liberal and Conservative agricultural experts who sat on both commissions; and Little, an assistant to the Richmond Commission and a member of its successor.

The Richmond Commission has been criticised on the grounds that it leaned too heavily on landlord opinion from the lowland zone, and paid too little attention to farmers from the north and west of England. The assertion contains some truth, though a long period was spent hearing Scottish and Irish evidence.[59] Internal politics are much more evident in the second Royal Commission than the first, culminating in the resignation of the Liberal chairman, G. J. Shaw-Lefevre, his acrimonious dispute with Chaplin on rating relief, and accusations that the new Conservative government was trying to force this proposal into the commission's report via Chaplin and Long.[60] A further consequence was a host of dissenting reports and reservations—'a discordant compendium of many voices'.[61] For example, Channing believed that the extent and severity of the depression had been underestimated,[62] and Everett favoured bimetallism.[63] It is only too easily forgotten that each Commission found substantial areas of agreement. The Richmond Commission put adverse seasons well up its list, and its successor stated that 'the evidence which has been brought before us has convinced us of the extreme gravity of the agricultural situation'.[64] The scholar will probably value the work of the itinerant assistant commissioners more highly than the reports or even the verbal evidence. Most of them were agricultural experts who kept politics rather in the background.[65] The Richmond Commission sent such experts all over Britain; the second Commission was more selective, even more expert, and at its best and worst—Pringle on parts of Essex—positively dramatic. The scholars' meat, however, is in the reports these assistants prepared, their notes of meetings with groups and individuals, and their collection of statistics.

A not inconsiderable body of legislation owes at least something to these Royal Commissions, to their searchings, and to their somewhat negative findings. Agriculture was derated by half, at least nominally, at the behest of a Royal Commission in 1896.[66] A wider range of legislation owes something to them but perhaps more to a wider public opinion—the Smallholdings Act of 1892 and its effective successor of 1907, the re-establishment of the Board of Agriculture in 1889,[67] and the provision of funds for agricultural education through such sources as the 'whiskey money' of 1890.[68] Much agricultural legislation was more directly political in its motivation, aiming to reduce landlord power and privilege, to strengthen the tenant's position and even to make him an owner. Some of this legislation had agrarian as well as political importance—the Agricultural Holdings Act of 1875 and 1883 gave a legal basis to tenant-right. Some other, such as the Ground Game Act of 1880, which allowed tenants to kill rabbits and hares, had much less. Perhaps the most surprising legislation of this kind was that passed by the Conservatives in 1888 to establish County Councils, which further, but by no means immediately, undermined the landlords' political power.[69] Some legislation turned out in the circumstances of the depression to favour the landowner, whatever its intention. One example was the Settled Lands Act of 1882, which facilitated land sales.[70] Finally farming used its own political institutions, such as the Central Chamber of Agriculture, founded in 1865, and its own 'politicians', such as Rew; they were in turn effective proponents of legislation on

Page 135

Sheep shearing, Nookton Farm, Co Durham, 1896. An obviously posed picture, perhaps the explanation of the numerous spectators. Technology remains primitive, the labour force large

Dairy class, Byton,
Herefordshire,
1907. Evidently
dairy work was
still women's work
despite its
unpopularity
among farmers'
wives and
daughters (see
p 115)

such matters as cattle imports, disease, and the adulteration of fertilisers and feeding stuffs.[71]

This legislation was useful, and much of it was long-lasting; but, as was only too evident to its recipients, it was no solution. 'They are in the nature of palliatives',[72] commented the second Royal Commission on its own suggestions; 'lois nouvelles . . . n'ont pu modifier que dans les détails très restreints les conditions économiques de l'industrie rurale',[73] commented one of the early French historians of the depression. It is nevertheless legitimate to ask what was the collective impact of these laws. How many personal tragedies were averted, how many new opportunities created? What desirable changes were fostered, how many worthy men were enabled to hang on? The evidence to answer these questions scarcely exists, but it is important to recognise the need for such questions when it is so easy to dismiss them as irrelevant.

Lastly there is the question of how the misfortunes of agriculture affected the political scene at large. The depression began and reached its first climax under a Conservative government, traditionally the landowners' and farmers' friend. That this government did nothing is scarcely surprising when the widespread ascription of blame for the depression on the seasons is considered. This point of view makes it the more surprising that Conservative losses at the 1880 general election could be blamed on the depression. So eminent an authority as Clark draws this conclusion,[74] although it was denied by Disraeli at the time and has been minimised in Lloyd's study of that election. Lloyd would point to the urban character of Liberal gains and to the part played by unofficial 'farmer liberal' candidates such as Duckham, who won the Herefordshire seat and whose detailed plans for agriculture contrasted with the mild and vague anti-landlord and pro-tenant party line.[75] Such a policy is spelled out in the third of Gladstone's Midlothian speeches, which begins on this theme so important to a rural audience, strongly favouring free trade and a tenantry free of restraints on energy and initiative.[76] It is echoed in Liberal editorials of the period.[77] The Liberals in power, however, were no more inclined to activism than their opponents, let alone to act on the radical views of Collings or Chamberlain. In fact some of the more radical measures came from

I

the Conservatives, who were more often in power after 1885—on the County Councils, for example. The flexibility of politics and politicians must not be forgotten; Chaplin could oppose smallholdings as 'socialistic' in 1886 and support them as 'conservative' in 1892.[78] Moreover agriculture remained political small beer by comparison with, say, Ireland or the Eastern Question.

Until early in this century the supreme step of a return to protection remained unthinkable; even landowners were too much involved in trade and industry to be eager for it. Paradoxically the involvement which impeded political action facilitated personal intervention: 'The interests of neither the aristocracy nor of the gentry were wholly identified with the fortunes of agriculture; and it probably made a very great difference to the social history of the country that when the fortunes of agriculture collapsed many of the great estates had other reasonably solid supports'.[79]

7

Conclusion

'SINCE 1862 THE tide of agricultural prosperity had ceased to
flow; after 1874 it turned, and rapidly ebbed.' Thus Ernle
commenced his chapter on the depression and initiated a continuing debate. How far does his version require modification?
In what ways is so simple and dramatic a model an oversimplification? Four directions suggest themselves for amplification—in time, in space, in perceptions and in participants.

But one among several turning points, 1874 was the last,
and exceptional, good year before an equally exceptional
series of bad seasons. As such it was well remembered, but
so was 1879, 'the beginning of the end for the real old-time
farmer',[1] and 1880, which stands out sharply as a year of
economic disaster succeeding the environmental and technical
tribulations of its immediate precursor. In the highland zone
1885 was a turning point towards yet harder times, whereas
in the lowland zone it was part of a phase of temporary and
illusory remission. Depression was no continuous and regular
downward movement but a series of painful adjustments and
occasional ameliorations whose spatial component appears to
be well known. The lowland arable farmer was more prone to
failure than the highland pastoralist; distance from urban
markets, the character of the soil, were likewise significant
factors, locally as well as nationally. But this, too, has been an
area of oversimplification. Fletcher's emphasis on the crucial
'distinction between the livestock farmer and the arable
farmer'[2] raises an exaggerated antithesis and ignores a degree
of symbiosis and a complex geography. Breeder and feeder

may be a more significant coupling. A contemporary commentator, Rew, expressed the distinction in the depression context quite accurately: 'The balance of power has shifted from the corn grower to the stock breeder and the dairy farmer'.[3]

Only when the situation is seen in the mind's eye of a late nineteenth-century farmer does the apparent anomaly of a depression, sharply differentiated in space and according to farming system but whose widespread existence was averred and assumed, become resolved. By comparison with past and personal experience nearly every British farmer fared worse after 1875 than before. Such comparison, over time rather than space, appears to have been the typical attitude, and complaint, of the farmer, though not of the 'expert', of the period. It coloured both his decision making, based as it was on scanty financial data, and his conversation.

For the landowner as for the farmer the depression was a serious and sustained loss of income and capital; it also entailed a loss of status, and a less attractive and often less active role in rural society. Extreme financial calamity might remove the farmer altogether from the farming ladder or, in not a few cases, it might force the landowner into non-residence. The labourer, however, was presented with a more open and accessible 'farming ladder' and higher real wages. At the same time a halt in the increase of money wages, a slight rise in rural unemployment, the wish of farmers to dispense with labour, and a variety of technical developments facilitated and encouraged rural out-migration.

An adequate overview of the depression must, then, bear in mind the existence of these four areas of more or less sharp differentiation which, in turn, summarise many of its important features. How far does such an overview conform to wider theories of agricultural change? Evidently the situation predicated by Firey was not reached: 'A break point . . . beyond which the new processes so far exceed social expectations that all dependability in people's behaviour breaks down'.[4] Only exceptionally was this the case in late nineteenth-century Britain—in parts of East Anglia, for example. Rather, new processes were examined and tested, accepted or rejected, first by a minority and then more widely, to be integrated to some degree into an existing body of farming knowledge and practice. The economic and technical value of resources was reassessed, but reversion to traditional valuations and old practices and preferences in even marginally more favourable circumstances was common. Change was reluctantly undertaken, innovation unwillingly accepted. Wolpert's stress on the role of capital in facilitating agricultural change explains much. The observation that 'the individual is adaptively or intendedly rational rather than omnisciently rational'[5] also rings true, notably in cereal growing and, as always, in the market place, for stores and fat beasts. The depression was less an overwhelming catastrophe than a series of difficult decisions taken by relatively isolated individuals in constrained economic and informational circumstances.

Change and decay are thus the salient components of the years of depression; neither alone adequately compares and contrasts the rural Britain of the 1870s with that of the 1900s, when a greener but more dilapidated Britain had arisen, employing fewer men more efficiently, and contributing to an improved diet for the British people. It had become a sea (not a desert) of generally extensive farming with islands (not oases) of intensive methods—an agrarian geography of sharpened differences and heightened contrasts.

The changes which took place were both deliberate and unplanned. Thus accelerated changes in the personnel of farming were an amalgam of both deliberate and avowedly rational decisions, and of unforeseen and unwelcome misfortunes. At the most local level the chance circumstances of landlord attitude and farmer skill and fortune were paramount in determining the degree and kind of such changes. At the regional and national level less random patterns, spatial and temporal, appear. Similarly grassland farming progressed in both ways: permanent pasture was laid down and systems of ley farming were developed at the same time as the acreage of 'tumbledown' grass increased. The increased importance of dairying for urban markets and changes in cropping, notably the expansion of horticulture, are better viewed in terms of deliberate decision and the seizing of favourable opportunity. Basic slag is a good instance of the latter—the potential, and more and more the actual, transformation of a problem situation by means of a fertiliser created as a by-product of technical advance in the iron and steel industry. Similarly horticulturalists seized the opportunity of cheap land in favourable locations.

Such developments took place in a broad context of financial weakness, often discussed at the time in its role as an inhibiting factor. Changes calling for substantial expenditure and long-term investment were not easily undertaken; neither confidence, nor credit, nor capital was readily available. The kind of gradual change which could be undertaken at minimal cost was favoured, such as a move from cereal cultivation to livestock on grass or towards catch cropping and even market gardening. Contemporary commentators took differing positions on this matter. Hall doubted 'if low prices and hard times ever make for improvement . . . the farmer sits tight and reduces what may already be an insufficient expenditure'.[6] While diversification was widely, though not universally, advocated, farmers and landowners disagreed about its practicability in their own locality and environment. Thompson has written of a 'short period from 1880 to 1914 . . . free from profound technical changes'.[7] Such an assertion is defensible only in terms of a narrow focus on traditional arable farming, a narrow interpretation of what is technical. It is to neglect pasture and ley, dairy and orchard. It must, however, be admitted that changes in outlook and attitude, slow and reluctant as they were, deserve a higher rating than technical developments. Two of these former deserve particular mention. Farming was seen more and more as a business—'Each year brings into clearer light and commercial basis of successful farming'[8]—to be planned and practised as such. The great commercialisation is a major component of the great depression. In this situation the future of British farming was seen to be closely linked with quality production and with those commodities, like fresh milk and fruit, where overseas competition was least likely.

The decay caused by the depression, which gives it its name, presents fewer problems. Lower prices, lower rents, diminished profit and reduced manpower were facts and circumstances of immediate contemporary comment and concern. 'Down corn—up horn.' The reality of their impact is widely attested and their spatial and sectoral characteristics have already been examined. Very largely the farmers' misfortunes, and those of the landowners, resulted from circumstances beyond their control—from price movements and adverse seasons. That these were widely misunderstood was a further characteristic of the depression. A realisation that the whole process might, *inter alia*, be realistically interpreted as the writing-off of an excessive capitalisation in changed economic circumstances, as the economic negation of the capital-intensive technical changes commonly called 'high farming', largely awaited the analyses of agricultural historians.[9] Contemporaries more often regarded lack of capital as a basic problem. In this as in so many other areas past experience provided an inadequate and unsuitable framework of assumptions within which to evaluate the situation.

Anomalous features, fitting aptly into neither the category of change nor of decay, are to be expected in a situation of clouded perception, limited rationality, and chance circumstance. The experience of thousands of farmers, and particularly of pioneers and innovators, refuses to be categorised and pigeon-holed. Dairy farming and orchards required not only new skills and attitudes but solid long-term investment. They progressed in an environment unfavourable in the latter respect solely because able and enthusiastic individuals found their way round this obstacle. Chaplin's observation that they were no universal panacea reflects the human as well as the commercial and environmental situation. An inherently less attractive anomaly is the continuing demand, often at high rents, for farms in the highland zone, a seeming irrationality which exacerbated depression in an otherwise relatively favourable situation. Again an element of personal commitment is evident in the decision to pay more, to accept a lower income, in order to remain in or enter farming in a particular locality.

As to the general context within which agricultural changes took place it must be recalled that the situation was one of apparently widespread economic problems. While Beales stressed the 'special character and causes'[10] of rural problems, Wilson has more recently presented a cogent revision of received versions of late nineteenth-century economic circumstances, aptly comparing the experience of agriculture and the rest of the economy as 'not a uniform tendency to move in one direction but a marked proclivity to move in several different directions at once'.[11] No doubt the late Victorian farmer and landowner had their belief in progress, perhaps already ebbing, severely pruned by their experiences. Progress has victims as well as beneficiaries. The middle and upper echelons of rural society were the victims of the need for a cheap food supply for the industrial labour force, basic to Britain's industrial expertise if no longer pre-eminence, and of the need to service British colonial and foreign investment.

But was the sacrifice, the victim, really necessary? German economic (and political) competition, a contemporary bogey, was built not upon cheap food but, inter alia, upon a united protectionist front of farmers and manufacturers.[12] In Britain industry played a less direct and political role, as Kitson Clark has pointed out, in enabling many landowners to remit or reduce rents, and in enabling redundant farm workers to find new jobs. Movement out of the industry, reluctant and at least temporarily uncomfortable, was the commonest alleviation of agricultural distress. In its reluctance to move or change, the farming and landed interest was commonly its own worst enemy. Contemporary criticism of this attitude is common—'Want of energy is the greatest evil among the farming interest'[13]—and is echoed by Clapham's assertion that it was 'impossible not to believe that . . . she (Britain) might have done better, if not with her grain crops under the system of free imports, at least with her cattle and pigs and fruit and poultry'.[14] The enervating effects of a period of easy prosperity, the educational deficiencies of the farming community, and its traditional attitudes conspired with such circumstances as adverse seasons to inhibit desirable changes.

The possible role of government action in this area is open to question. The legislation enacted was largely peripheral and palliative. Astor and Rowntree later claimed 'that at such times appropriate measures of assistance would have eased their position without any prejudice to the national welfare'.[15] Writing in the late 1930s while witnessing and sharing in the first wave of active peacetime government intervention in British agriculture since 1846, they offered no exact suggestions and may be accused of a somewhat euphoric misjudgement of late nineteenth-century conditions. Protection, advocated by more and more farmers, was unacceptable to the dominant political groups. Policies of intervention in markets, of support prices and subsidies, or of relief to rural debtors along lines pursued in New Zealand in the 1930s,[16] appear unthinkable in late Victorian Britain. Action had to be restricted to such areas as tenant-right and rural education. Even these were limited in their effectiveness by the reluctance of most farmers to change course. For this group no rapidly effective policy can be envisaged; for the dynamic minority none was needed.

This is not to argue that nothing about processes and patterns of change in farming of interest, in, say, the Common Market context is to be learned from an examination of what happened in Britain in the last quarter of the nineteenth century. Rather it is to admit that such *laissez-faire* change is economically and socially inefficient and indiscriminate; rural depopulation in peasant societies in postwar Europe provides a very close analogy in these respects. The depression was 'not a mere passing wave . . . but a permanent alteration in the relative position of the diverse industries of the country'.[17] This process of alteration and adjustment, containing a strong spatial component, is a continuing phenomenon, within farming, between farming and other sectors of the economy, and through the whole of economy and society. In exemplifying this phenomenon in an acute form, the 'great agricultural depression' provides no ideal model, no simple solution. There are none. Its investigation and understanding may yet serve to sharpen the critic's mind—perhaps, too, the planner's and the politician's—to enable him better to differentiate between practicable and impracticable, humane and inhumane, conservative and destructive uses of a rich variety of rural resources, for the last quarter of this as of the last century. To quote Edmund Burke: 'People will not look forward to posterity who never look backward to their ancestors.'[18]

Abbreviations

AgHR	*Agricultural History Review*
BPP	British Parliamentary Papers
DAP	Board of Agriculture and Fisheries: *Report on the Decline in the Agricultural Population of Great Britain 1881–1906*
EcHR	*Economic History Review*
EJ	*Economic Journal*
FI	Departmental Committee appointed by the Board of Agriculture and Fisheries to enquire into and report upon the Fruit Industry of Great Britain 1905
HAS	*Transactions of the Highland and Agricultural Society*
JRASE	*Journal of the Royal Agricultural Society of England*
JRSS	*Journal of the Royal Statistical Society*
IBG	Institute of British Geographers: *Transactions* and *Papers*
RC1	Royal Commission on the Depressed Condition of Agricultural Interests 1880–82 (the 'Richmond Commission')
RC2	Royal Commission on the Agricultural Depression 1894–97
RCL	Royal Commission on Labour 1892–94
VCH	*Victoria County History*
WLC	Royal Commission on Land (Wales and Monmouthshire) 1894–96

Notes and References

Chapter 1   The Context of the Depression

1   The best known revisions are Chambers and Mingay, *The Agricultural Revolution 1750–1880* (1966); Kerridge, *The Agricultural Revolution* (1967); Jones, E. L. (ed) *Agriculture and Economic Growth in England 1650–1815* (1967)

2   For example, by Jones, Collins, Sturgess and Phillips in the *Agricultural History Review* between 1963 and 1969

3   The best examples are in *Hodge and his Masters* (1880) in such pieces as 'Going Downhill' and 'Mademoiselle, the Governess'. (Where possible in these notes Jefferies' individual essays have been dated.) See also Perry, 'Richard Jefferies', *Journal of British Studies, 9* (1970), 126–40

4   Saul, *The Myth of the Great Depression* (1969), 34–6

5   Law, 'The growth of Urban Population in England and Wales, 1801–1911', *IBG*, 41 (1967), 125–43; Ojala, *Agriculture and Economic Progress* (1953), 84

6   For a broad comparison of the reaction of western European countries to late nineteenth-century circumstances and since, see Tracy, *Agriculture in Western Europe: crisis and adaptation since 1880* (1964)

7   Clark, *The Making of Victorian England* (1962), 216

8   Perry, 'Working-class isolation and mobility in rural Dorset, 1837–1936: a study of marriage distances', *IBG*, 46 (1969), 121–42

9   Dunbabin, 'The incidence and oganisation of agricultural trades unionism in the 1870s', *AgHR*, 16 (1968), 114–41

10 The Agricultural Holdings Act of 1875 gave legal recognition to the tenant's right to compensation for certain classes of improvements. Such recognition had commonly been customary. Many

147

landlords contracted out of the 1875 Act, which was often for this reason referred to as 'a homily to landlords'; later legislation, notably in 1883, made the Act compulsory and stopped up other loopholes

11 Smallholdings Acts were passed in 1892 and 1908, the latter being much the more effective

12 The important advances in the manufacture of tile drains date from the late 1830s and early 1840s. See Darby, 'The drainage of the English claylands', *Geographische Zeitschrift*, 52 (1964) 194–6. The Public Money Drainage Act was passed in 1846, and several drainage companies were set up as a result

13 These are the official Corn Returns prices collected at the principal markets, published in the *London Gazette,* and reprinted in *A Century of Agricultural Statistics,* 81–2. Cereal prices were sometimes quoted in quarters (of 8 bushels or about 540lb), sometimes in cwt; for comparison wheat was 17s 5d (87p) per cwt in 1855, 15s (75p) in 1867. (Note the 28lb quarter was not used for wheat.)

14 Besse, *La crise et l'évolution d'agriculture en Angleterre* (1910), 347; deriving his figures, applying to sixty-nine farms in England and Wales, from *RC1*

15 Thompson, 'An enquiry into the rent of agricultural land', *JRSS*, 70 (1907), 587–616

16 Rew, *Agricultural Faggot* (1913), 31. In this chapter Rew takes the unusual and interesting course of treating the period 1846–96 as a whole

17 Jones, 'The changing basis of English agricultural prosperity' *AgHR*, 10 (1963), 102–19

18 Cornish, *Reminiscences* (1939), 83

19 A common complaint by Richard Jefferies: 'Has not some of the old stubborn spirit of earnest work and careful prudence gone with the advent of the piano and the oil painting'. See 'The Fine Lady Farmer—Country Girls', in *Hodge and his Masters* (1880). Farmers' wives and daughters were usually regarded as the chief culprits

20 Caird, *The Landed Interest and the Supply of Food* (1878, reprinted 1967), 28

21 The Isle of Axholme was one such area; a heavy burden of mortgage indebtedness made its position particularly difficult during the depression. See Hunter Pringle's report, *RC2* (1894), XVI, pt 1, 671–96

22 Hence, inter alia, the need for *WLC*, which heard a great deal of evidence on these matters, much less frequently discussed elsewhere in Britain

23 Spring, *English Landed Estate in the Nineteenth Century* (1963), 108–9

24 According to C. S. Read, Lord Leicester once had a list of 300 prospective tenants. See *RC2*, Q16601

25 Many sheep-breed societies in Britain date from the depression rather than the high farming period, although show classes are generally older. Thus the Suffolk society was set up in 1886, the Oxford in 1888. Stevens, *Sheep*, Pt 2, 146 and 179

26 Howard, *JRASE*, 16 (1880), 436

27 Ashby, *Joseph Ashby of Tysoe*, 89–90

28 A Leicestershire comment, quoted by Druce, 'Report on Eastern Counties', *RC1* (1882), XV, 298

29 Fussell, *English Dairy Farmer*, 169, relating the issue also to long working hours and to prosperity engendered by the Napoleonic war

30 For full discussion see Fussell, *English Dairy Farmer*; and Whetham, 'Changing cattle enterprise', *Geographical Journal*, 129 (1963), and 'London milk trade', *EcHR*, 17 (1964–5). Dairyman Crick in *Tess of the D'Urbervilles* (c 1880) sent milk to London and made butter and cheese, probably a common situation

31 Jefferies, 'The Dairy' (probably 1877), *Field and Farm*; he also noted the replacement of unsuccessful local cheese makers by Somerset men with a tradition of quality cheese making

32 The mainstay of many Scottish migrants, and one of Strutt's enterprises. See *RC2* and Gavin, passim

33 Graham, *Revival of English agriculture*, 263; *Fussell, English Dairy Farmer*, 310–32

34 The most notable of these was tomato growing, although the tomato was as yet scarcely a popular vegetable. See Wheadon, 'History and cultivation of the tomato in Guernsey', *La Société Guernsiaise—Transactions*, 12 (1935), 337

35 Venn, *Agricultural Economics*, 12–13

36 *RC1*, Q55336, a tenant farmer from Cottenham, Cambridgeshire; at Q45307 (and elsewhere) emulation of gardening is advocated as a solution for problems of the depression

37 Eagle, 'The Spalding bulb industry', *Lincs Historian*, 6 (1950), 220–9; Pratt, *Transition in Agriculture* (1906), 98–132, with references to similar developments in Middlesex and Bedfordshire

38 For example, Evesham custom; see note 86, Chapter 2

39 *FI* (1905), XX, 546

40 Rew, 'Heathfield', *RC2*, 1895, XVI, 445–76; it is of interest to note that one of the early centres of broiler production in Britain, at Buxted, is in the same district

41 Walker, 'Report on Northern Scotland', *RC1* (1881), XVI, 536. Letting by tender, generally more common in the highland zone, elevated rents (*RC1*, Q44667–8) and encouraged farmers to run down at the end of their lease. See Maxton, *Landownership in Scotland*, 23–4

42 Devon and Cornwall provided almost a quarter of assisted emigrants to Canterbury province, New Zealand, between 1853 and 1876, a prosperous period for British farming.

43 Smith, *Go East for a Farm* (1932)

44 Orr, *Oxfordshire*, 232–5

45 In parts of the highland zone they increased. See Fletcher, 'Lancashire Livestock farming', *AgHR*, 9 (1961), 33–5

46 Hunt, 'Labour productivity in English agriculture 1850–1914', *EcHR*, 20 (1967), 280–92

47 Perry, 'Where was the "Great Agricultural Depression"', *AgHR*, 20 (1972), 30–45

48 Olson and Harris, 'Free trade in "corn"', *Quarterly Journal of Economics*, 73 (1959), 147–68

49 *Bedfordshire Times and Independent* and *Westmorland Gazette and Kendal Advertiser,* advertisement columns

50 Perry and Johnston, 'The temporal and spatial incidence of agricultural depression', *Journal of Interdisciplinary History*, 3 (1972), 297–311

51 Hall, *Pilgrimage of British Farming*, 145–54, in summarising the first part of his pilgrimage

52 Hall, 250

53 King and Arch, 'Statistics of some Midland villages', *EJ*, 3 (1893), 22

54 Thompson, *VCH Wilts*, IV, 92–114 ; Perren 'Landlord and agricultural transformation', *AgHR*, 18 (1970)

55 Perry and Johnston, *Journal of Interdisciplinary History*, 3 (1972), 297–311

56 For example, C. S. Read before *RC2*: 'We have not had an all-round good crop of farm produce since the year 1874' (Q15952). In fact such years are rare in Britain ; 1874 was a dry summer made memorable by the wet summers which followed

57 Jones, 'The changing basis of English agricultural prosperity 1853–1873', *AgHR*, 10 (1962), 102–19

58 Ralston, 'Agriculture of Wigstownshire', *HAS* 1 (1885), notes a fall from 64s–68s to 36s–40s (£3·2–£3·4 to £1·8–£2)

59 Smith, *No rain in these clouds*, 21–5, in discussing 1878 and 1879. In haymaking 1879 'the horses shied at the water standing in the grass'

60 Ricks, C. (ed), *The Poems of Tennyson* (1969), 1,260

61 *RC1*, Q62647 ; James Caird
62 For example *RC1*, Q36276
63 *RC1*, Q30554, Druce, assistant commissioner in the eastern counties included 'high rates, school-board rates, compulsory education' in the tenor of complaints. On the railway-rates issue several railway managers were called before *RC1*—eg on 3 June 1880 the General Manager of the LNWR and the Assistant Goods Manager of the Great Northern
64 W. C. Cartwright, MP, at the fiftieth anniversary of Banbury Agricultural Society (*Banbury Guardian*, 20 January 1880) ; quoted by Taylor, *Gillett's*, 173–4
65 Notably *WLC*, eg Q9530. One witness observed (Q29822) that landlords only began to recognise the depression in 1885, whereas it had been a reality to farmers from 1879
66 Rew, 'Norfolk', *RC2*, 1895, XVII, 332
67 Walker, *Farming to Profit*, introduction
68 Venn, *Agricultural Economics*, 555 ; the 10 year moving average of wheat yields rose from 26 bushels per acre in 1880 to 28·8 by 1890. This latter is no higher than the moving average for 1858–67, but by 1894 30 bushels was exceeded. No one year compared with 1863, when the yield was 38·7 bushels (see Fig 14 p 55)
69 Thompson, *JRSS*, 70 (1907), 614
70 *RC1*, Q34838–42
71 *RC2*, Q13876. But Strutt admitted (Q13812) that, except for 1893, he had made 6 per cent plus rent (of 17s to 18s or 85p to 90p) on his capital
72 Stamp, *British Incomes and Property* (1916), Table A4, 49
73 Publicised above all by Pringle, 'Ongar etc', *RC2* (1894), XVI, Pt 1, 697–801 ; correctives are Matthews' evidence, 8 November 1895, Q61453 ('The district where I reside is farmed pretty well, and no farm is out of cultivation there'), and Smith, *No rain in these clouds*
74 Graham, *Revival of English Agriculture,* 91–100
75 Thompson's rent index, *JRSS*, 70 (1907), reached its minimum of 70 (1872=103) as late as 1904 ; cereal prices rose after the mid-1890s
76 Hall, *Pilgrimage of British farming* (1913), 6
77 For example, Hall, 145–54, evidently rather to the author's surprise in some respects ; Street, *Farmer's Glory* (1932), Part 1
78 Layton and Crowther, *The Study of Prices,* 229–31
79 Basic slag, a by-product of the Gilchrist-Thomas process of steel manufacture perfected in 1879, thus became available to farmers in the 1880s and commonplace in the 1890s

Chapter 2　Causes of the Depression

1　Jones, 'Changing basis of English agricultural prosperity', *AgHR*, 10 (1962), 102–19

2　Note that cereal prices did not collapse during the first period of acute depression, and that the price of wheat fell less rapidly than the price of barley or oats at this date

3　Olson and Harris, 'Free trade in "corn" ', *Quarterly Journal of Economics*, 73 (1959) notes this trend (154–5). Whereas in 1874 there were 3·63 million acres of wheat and 2·29 of barley, in 1894 there were 1·93 and 2·10 respectively. Others found substitution difficult, eg *RC1* Q52986 (Fens)

4　Noted as early as 1879. See Savory, *Grain and Chaff*, 245

5　Malden, 'The Greater Agriculture', *Nineteenth Century and After*, 437 (July 1913), 100

6　Long et al. *Handbook for Farmers* (1892), 7

7　Shannon, *The Farmer's Last Frontier, Agriculture 1860–1897*, 181–2

8　The high price was given by Beadel, a surveyor, Q4915 ; the lowest by Bowen Jones, a north Shropshire farmer (Q33451–2), but not for a purely arable farm. The prophet of gloom (Q37260–1) was Cowan, a Wigtownshire farmer who believed that 48s (£2·40) was the lowest profitable price

9　McConnell, 'Experiences of a Scotsman', *JRASE*, 2 (1891), 320.

10　Savory, *Grain and Chaff*, 208, notes the continuance of cereal growing on a reduced scale for straw in Worcestershire ; Rew, 'Agricultural situation in the west', *Journal of the Bath and West*, 5 (1894–5) notes the importance of oats on large farms in Dorset and Wiltshire

11　*RC1*, Q47966 (Pringle on Essex)

12　*RC2*, Q13094 et seq

13　Little, 'Report on Southern Counties', *RC1*, 1882, XV, 33

14　Thompson, *VCH Wilts*, IV, 109

15　Jessopp, *Arcady*, 200

16　The final report of *RC2* gives 25–33 per cent for 1874–91 and 16 per cent for butter for 1876–8 to 1892–4. Fletcher, 'Lancashire Livestock Farming', *AgHR*, 9 (1961), suggests stable fresh milk prices

17　Garnett, *Westmorland Agriculture*, 139–40

18　Scots and Derbyshire witnesses often commented thus to *RC1*, eg Cowan, 7 April 1881, and Coleman, 13 May 1881

19   Jefferies, 'Haymaking—"The Juke's Country"', *Hodge and His Masters* (1880)

20   Moore, 'The winter of 1885–86', *JRASE*, 22 (1886), 440, mentions wheat and advocates silage and brewers' grains. See also *RC2*, Q6471

21   See notes 88 and 89

22   Murray, *Factors affecting the price of Livestock*, 49–64

23   Sauerbeck's price index (1867–77=100) reached a low of 62 for food in 1896, and 59 for raw materials in 1897. *The Economist* index stood at around 130 in 1872–4, and at a low of 86 in 1898 (1945–50=100), Layton and Crowther, *The Study of Prices* (1935), 225–35

24   Besse, 41–117, discusses falling prices

25   Hutcheson, 'The past and future of Scottish agriculture', *HAS*, 11 (1899), 127; refuted anonymously, 'The economic effects of cattle disease legislation', *EJ*, 15 (1905), 156–63

26   Fletcher, *AgHR*, 9 (1961), 31

27   Wilson, 'Half a century as a Border farmer', *HAS*, 15 (1902), 35–48

28   Bear, 'Agricultural Problem', *EJ*, 3 (1893), 575

29   Besse, 31

30   Stevens, *Sheep*, Pt 2, 31–2

31   Besse, 32

32   Clapham, *Economic History of Modern Britain*, II, 282

33   Conacher, 'Causes of the fall in agricultural prices', *Scottish Journal of Agriculture*, 19 (1936), 239–47

34   Chaplin was among those favouring bimetallism—see a supplementary report to *RC2* (1897), XV, 160–72 Giffen's evidence was given on 26 April 1894, his memorandum being in *RC2*, XV, 173–7

35   Wrightson, *Livestock*, 137, claimed that sheep were sometimes deliberately rotted to accelerate fattening

36   Hutcheson, 127

37   Murray, 49–64 and 100–4

38   For example, Fussell, 'Cornish Farming', *Amateur Historian*, 4 (1960), 343–4, notes how little Cornish livestock was affected. For Highlands see *RC1*, Q43444

39   Symons, 'Recent British weather', *JRASE*, 19 (1883), 411–21

40   *RC1*, Q62674

41   *RC1*, Q57060

42   Stanton Diaries, Bedfordshire Record Office, CRT 160/54D

43   *RC1*, Q46538

44   Fussell, 'Four centuries of farming systems in Shropshire', *Trans Salop Arch Soc*, 54 (1953), 1–29

K

45 'Part of the wheat proved so poor that they could not sell it at market . . . ground at the village mills . . . the flour was so bad as to be unpalatable', Jefferies, *Round About a Great Estate* (1880), Chapter 9

46 Since wet years were weedy years; such a failure acted over several subsequent years

47 Bedford, *A Great Agricultural Estate* (1897), 187

48 Jefferies, 'Nutty Autumn' (1881), *Nature Near London* (1883)

49 *RC1*, Q6342 and elsewhere in J. Denton's evidence, 14 May 1880

50 *RC1*, Q4750

51 Perren, 'Landlord and agricultural transformation', *AgHR*, 18 (1970)

52 Gavin, 76, notes that draining was the one area where Strutt was prepared to spend money

53 Little, 'Report on Southern Counties', *RC1* (1881), XVI, 398. See also Kendall, *Farming Memoirs*, 107

54 Pringle, 'Bedfordshire etc', *RC2* (1895), XVII, 14

55 *RC1*, Q34778

56 Trow-Smith, *British Livestock Husbandry*, 317–18

57 *RC1*, Q45144

58 Hall, *Pilgrimage of British Farming*, 91–2; as a result potato growing passed into the hands of large farmers

59 *Fasciola Hepatica*. For discussion of the epidemic see, inter alia, Dun, 'Report on Liver rot', *JRASE*, 17 (1881), 141–204. Even cattle suffered, *RC1*, Q1822

60 Dun, 199

61 Little, 'Report on Southern Counties', *RC1* (1881), XVI, 397

62 Ibid, 437

63 Perry, 'Where was the "Great Agricultural Depression"', *AgHR*, 20 (1972), Map VII

64 Jefferies, 'Spring Prospects and Farm Work' (1878), *Chronicles of the Hedges*

65 *RC2*, Q47503. The witness was Pringle, the Assistant Commissioner who investigated the most depressed eastern districts

66 Little, 'Report on Southern Counties', *RC1* (1881), XVI, 398

67 Coleman, 'Report on Northern Counties', *RC1* (1881), XVI, 228

68 Kendall, 125–6

69 But statements of the position usually emphasise the problems of poor heavy or light land, eg *RC1*, Q2446

70 Bedford, 1880

71 Implicit in many assertions that seasons were the main cause, eg *RC1*, Q37442

72 Bear, 'Agricultural Problem', *EJ*, 3 (1893), 573

73 And harder to collect; Jefferies, 'Haymaking—"The Juke's Country" ', *Hodge and His Masters* (1880)

74 Wilson Fox, 'Lincolnshire', *RC2* (1895), XVI, 155

75 The minority report is in *RC2* (1896), XVI, 434–43, signed by Shaw-Lefevre, Giffen and Lord Rendel. There is correspondence on the matter in *The Times* (27 April to 1 May 1896)

76 *RC2* (1896), XVI, 443–57 for Shaw-Lefevre, 424–9 and passim for majority

77 Jefferies, 'The Squire and the Land' (1878?), *The Old House at Coate*

78 *WLC*, Q71398

79 Thus, early in the depression, eg *RC1*, Q40626, permanent reductions are asked for or advocated, but abatements are more common.

80 Maxton, *Landownership in Scotland*, 157

81 See, for example, evidence of W. Smith, MP, and T. Parker, *RC2* (23 February and 2 March 1894)

82 Demonstrated by Thompson, 'Enquiry into the rent of agricultural land', *JRSS*, 70 (1907), 587–616

83 Morton, 'The past agricultural year', *JRASE*, 16 (1880), 248; also *RC1*, Q466 and 32975

84 Walker, 'Report on Northern Scotland', *RC1* (1881), XVI, 549 (Fife)

85 Rowe, 'Cornish Agriculture', *Journal Royal Institution Cornwall,* 3 (1957–60), 151 ; a case of letting by tender

86 In fruit districts tenant-right was usually very favourable, as at Evesham where the outgoer virtually found a successor to buy him out. *See FI* (1905), XX, 15

87 *RC2*, Q1416–17 (Yorkshire Wolds)

88 Discussed at *RC1*, Q32670–5 and *RC2*, Q9612

89 Wilson Fox, 'Lincolnshire', *RC2* (1895), XVI, 156

90 Rew, *Agricultural Faggot*, 141–58

91 Ibid, estimating 45s (£2.25) per head on fat stock sold, and 20s (£1) on stores purchased

92 Little, 'Report on Southern Counties', *RC1* (1881), XVI, 398; Hammond, *Livestock changes in Norfolk*, 11. But a witness before *RC2*, Q54757, noted that this was not an inherently bad practice

93 Kerr, *Bound to the Soil*, 245–7. The Symonds, Ensor and Duke families are mentioned ; they remain active in this role

94 Besse, 117

95 For the decline of this national and regional differentiation

see Hunt, 'Labour productivity, 1850–1914', *EcHR*, 20 (1967)

96 Ojala, 153
97 Various authorities discuss this relationship. *DAP* equates loss of 2 million arable acres with 60,000 to 80,000 labourers (1906, XCVI, 593). See also Chapter 6
98 Evans and Bowstead, 'Laying down land to permanent pasture', *JRASE*, 11 (1875), 448
99 Coleman, 'Report on Northern Counties', *RC1* (1881), XVI, 143
100 Olson and Harris, 'Free trade in "corn"', *Quarterly Journal of Economics*, 73 (1959), 165–6
101 Astor and Rowntree, *British Agriculture*, 64

Chapter 3 Landowners and the Depression

1 *WLC* (1896), XXXIV, 582, gives a minimum figure of 85 per cent for England and a maximum of 88 per cent for Wales within Great Britain
2 A land reform slogan popularised by the radical Jesse Collings in 1885
3 Kitson Clark, *Making of Victorian England*, 216
4 Particularly in the relatively more prosperous north-western counties: for example, *RC2* evidence of J. Kay and J. Barlow, 26 March 1894. Among contemporary writers who thought landlord policies to be a big element in farmers' problems, Channing (*Truth about the Agricultural Depression*) was a member of *RC2*
5 Thompson, *VCH Wilts*, IV, 95, with respect to the Wilton estates
6 On the Weld (Lulworth, Dorset) estate, eight of thirty-one tenants had given notice to quit at Michaelmas 1879, but five of these were negotiating for a lower rent and were thought likely to succeed in this. Dorset Record Office, Weld papers, Rent accounts, etc, AE89–139
7 *RC1*, Q34297 quoted by a Lichfield tenant farmer
8 *RC1*, Q43293–301 (Aberdeenshire)
9 Oxley Parker, *Oxley Parker Papers*, 152
10 On the Bedford estate the substantial revaluation came only as late as 1895 (see text below)
11 *RC2*, Q48111–12 and 48135–6
12 Fream, 'Andover and Maidstone', *RC2* (1894), XVI, Pt 1, 499
13 Beastall, 'South Yorkshire Estate', *AgHR*, 14 (1966), 42, noted

the selective use of reductions to encourage good tenants from 1885. The receipt of better terms by new tenants than established ones is commented upon in *RC2*, Q9705

14 Orr, *Oxfordshire*, 85
15 Ibid
16 Hope, 'Roxburgh, etc', *RC2* (1895), XVII, 583–6. The role of cheap family labour was also noted
17 Conversely rents were commonly lowered for new tenants when maintained for old, *RC2*, Q41540
18 Thompson, *VCH Wilts,* IV, 104 ; Little, 'Report on Southern Counties', *RC1* (1881), XVI, 398
19 Little, 'Report on Southern Counties', *RC1* (1881), XVI, 398
20 Pringle, 'Isle of Axholme', *RC2* (1894), XVI, Pt 1, 683
21 Thus on some of the Weld rent accounts (Dorset Record Office AE89–139) the words 'subject to corn average' appear
22 Perren, 'The Landlord and Agricultural Transformation', *AgHR*, 18 (1970), 44–5, notes that drainage investment on the Sutherland Shropshire estates kept up rents until the 1890s
23 *RC2*, Q4405
24 *RC2,* Q6013, on the Duchy of Cornwall estates
25 For example, on the Constable estates in the East Riding substantial repairs required the owner's personal sanction from 1885, but expenditure was maintained on the nearby Sledmere estates ; Ward, *East Yorkshire Landed Estates*, 24 and 14
26 Duke of Bedford, *A Great Agricultural Estate* (1897), 113–27
27 Bedfordshire Record Office, Chicksands Estate, disbursements, rents, etc, 1872–81 (0158) and 1881–88 (0159). The area involved was about 1,350 acres
28 Vincent, *Land question in North Wales* (1896), 265–313. Pro-landlord
29 *WLC* (1896), XXXIV, 397
30 *RC1*, Q86
31 Caird, 'General View of British Agriculture', *JRASE*, 14 (1878), 315 ; Clapham, *Economic History of Modern Britain*, II, 278–9. Both note a greater increase in north and west despite lower levels of investment
32 Harvey, *History of Farm Buildings,* 118–58, aptly subtitled 'The industrial phase'
33 *RC2*, Q51180, respecting Scotland
34 Speir, 'Ayr, etc', *RC2* (1895), XVII, 525 ; Walker, 'Report on Northern Scotland', *RC1* (1881), XVI, 530 ; and more generally
35 Walker, 'Report on Northern Scotland', *RC1* (1881), XVI, 545 ; Doyle, 'Report on Midland Counties', *RC1* (1881), XVI, 281

36 *RC2*, Q3514 and 3527

37 *RC2*, 1812 and 1877

38 Fletcher, 'Lancashire Livestock Farming', *AgHR*, 9 (1961), 33

39 *WLC* (1896), XXXIV, 401. It was also noted that rents were more often raised on purchased than inherited estates

40 *RC2*, Q24379. The witness, A. Hutcheson, also wrote a shrewd essay on Scottish farming, *HAS*, 11 (1899), 121–35

41 Channing, 6, but no location is given. The value suggested is £5·60 per acre. The Duke of Bedford spent up to £10 per acre grassing down, *A Great Agricultural Estate*, 204

42 Channing, 3

43 Druce, 'Report on Eastern Counties', *RC1* (1882), XV, 280

44 *RC2*, Q10784 ; Rew, 'North Devon', *RC2* (1895), XVI, 11

45 Anderson, *VCH Glos*, II, 261

46 *WLC* index (1896), XXXV, 746, has some fifteen references to land going out of cultivation

47 A Cheshire tenant in evidence to *RC2* noted the absence of general rent reductions (Q22002), continuing competition for farms (Q22008), and his own satisfaction with a 10 per cent remission (Q22264)

48 *RC2*, Q49147. The witness was Rew, who reported on the county for the commission

49 *RCL*, 'Melton Mowbray' (1893–4), XXXV, 134 ; *RC2*, Q13330–1 and 20960 and 21020. Different time periods may also be involved

50 Thirsk, *English peasant farming . . . Lincolnshire*, 320

51 For example, in Sussex (Ingram, *VCH Sussex*, II, 286), comparing the Downs and the Weald. Spring, *English Landed Estate*, 108–9, notes that this was a perennial problem. It was also one of the circumstances enabling a small number of ambitious men to build up large multiple tenancies

52 Dulac, *Agriculture et libre-échange* (1903), 28

53 Thompson, *JRSS*, 70 (1907), 587–616

54 Maxton, *Landownership in Scotland*, 62, 55

55 Buckle, *VCH Dorset*, II, 276

56 Wilson Fox, 'Cumberland', *RC2*, 1895, XVII, 461

57 Thompson, 'Land market in the nineteenth century', *Oxford Economic Papers*, 9 (1957), 305

58 Ward, *East Yorkshire Landed Estates*, 41. Land was sold in 1890, 1894, 1898 and 1902, pictures in 1891. The role of previous surpluses in balancing the books is also noted

59 Beastall, 'South Yorkshire Estate', *AgHR*, 14 (1966), 41

60 Thompson, *Oxford Economic Papers*, 9 (1957), 285–308

61 *RC2*, Q8667–8, not a bankruptcy

62 *Dorset County Chronicle*, 13 May 1897. As far as I know this failure has not been the subject of substantial research

63 Ward, 'Farm sale prices', *Estates Gazette* (centennial supplement), 171 (1958), 49

64 'What between the duties expected of one during one's lifetime and the duties exacted from one after one's death land has ceased to be either a profit or a pleasure. It gives one position and prevents one from keeping it up.' *The Importance of Being Earnest* (1895), Act 1. (Harcourt's budget of 1894 first introduced death duties.) I am grateful to the late T. W. Fletcher for drawing my attention to this passage

65 Rew, 'Norfolk', *RC2* (1895), XVII, 344 (footnote): 'If you own land and have a grudge against a man, die and leave him a farm!'

66 Wilson Fox, 'Cumberland', *RC2* (1895), XVII, 485 ; Thompson, *English Landed Society* (1963), 317–18

67 Little, 'Report on Southern Counties', *RC1* (1881), XVI, 417, writing of cheese-making districts, cheese prices having fallen sharply

68 MacDonald, 'Agriculture of Selkirk', *HAS*, 18 (1886), 103

69 Garnett, *Westmorland Agriculture,* 235

70 *RC2*, Q46406. Unfortunately no dates are given. Parish by parish lists of changes appear in some Assistant Commissioners' reports, eg Rew, 'North Devon', *RC2* (1895), XVI, 47–8

71 Graham, *Revival of English Agriculture*, 202–10

72 Eagle, 'Lincolnshire bulb industry', *Lincolnshire Historian*, 6 (1950), 220–9

73 *FI* (1905), XX, 4

74 One of the best known and most often quoted aphorisms— 'well nigh strangled Suffolk'—occurs in Wilson Fox, 'Suffolk', *RC2* (1895), XVII, 392

75 In 1879 Jefferies wrote: 'In some fields the weeds are so thick that even a pheasant can hide' ('Midsummer 1879', *Chronicles of the Hedges*). This was the result of a succession of wet summers and of labour economies

76 Spier, 'Ayr, etc', *RC2* (1895), XVII, 528, notes that in the Machars (Wigtownshire) one-third of all tenancy changes since 1880 were due to tenants leaving their farms without means

77 Duke of Bedford, *A Great Agricultural Estate* (1897), 190, quotes from his agent's report on one farm: 'Dirty, in ordinary circumstances I should not hesitate advising a landlord to give such a tenant as Mr Z notice to quit'.

78 MacGregor, *History of Landownership since 1870*, 134

79 *RC1*, Q36010. Lack of capital was commonly regarded as a

problem in this context (Q4414–16) ; a few shrewd men realised the role of overcapitalisation later in the depression (*RC2*, Q17748)

80 Marchioness of Londonderry, *Henry Chaplin* (1926), 97–8. See also Chapter 6

81 Advertisement columns, *Dorset County Chronicle, Peterborough Advertiser*. See also Chapter 4

82 Rew, 'Dorset', *RC2* (1895), XVII, 255

83 Coleman, 'Report on Northern Counties', *RC1* (1882), XV, 635, referring to the Duke of Northumberland's estates ; Druce, 'Report on Eastern Counties', *RC1* (1881), XVI, 372 ; *RC1*, Q34095, but this witness observed that 3 years earlier, in 1878, more farms had been in hand

84 Bradley, *When Squires and Farmers thrived* (1927), 86

85 *Oxley Parker Papers*, 133 ; Ashby, *Joseph Ashby of Tysoe*, 75

86 *Dorset County Chronicle*. Some farms were advertised during several years, eg Rye Close and Willow Tree Farms, Folke, from 1880 to 1883. On other occasions several farms on the same estate would be advertised simultaneously, as were seven on Earl Sandwich's Hooke estate, for entry at Lady Day 1893

87 *RC1*, Q50440

88 Druce, 'Report on Eastern Counties', *RC1* (1881), XVI, 370

89 *RC1*, Q50378

90 Little, 'Report on Southern Counties', *RC1* (1881), XVI, 437. Little gained this information at a meeting with farmers on 9 April 1880 ; most Commissioners held such meetings

91 Druce, 'Report on Eastern Counties', *RC1* (1882), XV, 348. The Ground Game Act giving the tenant certain rights to destroy game was passed only in 1880

92 *RC2*, Q54. The Commissioner, Sir Robert Kingscote, was a member of both Royal Commissions

93 Perry, 'Where was the "Great Agricultural Depression"?', *AgHR*, 20 (1972), maps III and V (see Figs 1 and 2, pp 26 and 28)

94 *RC1*, Q990, 1044 and 1062

95 Pringle, 'Ongar, etc', *RC2* (1894), XVI, Pt 1, 704

96 'Almost everything will . . . depend on the class of soil', Ibid ; *RC2*, Q61453 and 61516

97 *RC2*, Q58047 (Merionethshire): Walker, 'Report on Northern Scotland' (1881), XVI, 552 (Dunbartonshire)

98 Wilson Fox, 'Suffolk', *RC2* (1895), XVI, 311, believed 4,700 acres to be totally derelict in that depressed county of nearly 800,000 acres in 1895

99 The definition problem is treated by Coppock in 'Statistical assessment of British agriculture', *AgHR*, 4 (1956), 4–21 and

66–79, and 'Agricultural Returns', *Amateur Historian*, 4 (1958–9), 49–55. There is no doubt that it caused much confusion at the time

100 Duke of Bedford, 180 ; this loss was on nine Bedfordshire farms of 200 to 490 acres

101 *RC2*, Q13812. Gavin, *Ninety Years of Family Farming*, Chapter six, is a detailed discussion

102 *RC2*, Q34592

103 Gavin, 81–3

104 His activities are reviewed by Lady Wantage, *Lord Wantage* (1907), and Havinden, *Estate Villages* (1967)

105 In the *Dorset County Chronicle* particularly numerous between 1889 and 1891, and 1896 and 1898

106 Duke of Bedford, 204

107 *RC1*, Q32636–9

108 Hence the appearance in advertisements of farms to let in the *Dorset County Chronicle* of such phrases as 'the quantity of arable land can be reduced if desired' and '24 acres only in arable'

109 Thompson, 'English Great Estates', *First Int Conf Econ Hist* (1960), 394–5

110 Personal communication from the Bedfordshire County Archivist. The steward's accounts for the estate, near Sandy, are of some interest (Bedfordshire Record Office, X344/2–10)

111 Havinden, Chapters 3 and 4. Economies of scale and management were one aim, made possible by increasing acreage in hand

112 Stapledon and Davies, *Ley Farming,* 15–18. Elliott is not listed in the *Dictionary of National Biography*

113 See, for example, Smyth, *HAS* 10 (1878), 'On the comparative return from capital', 255–75 arguing that forestry gives the best return on poor land

114 Ashworth, *Economic History of England*, 65–6

115 Wingfield-Stratford, *The Squire and his relations*, 404–5

116 Thompson, *Lark Rise to Candleford* (World's Classics), 543

117 Graham, *Revival of English Agriculture*, 95, cites a Cotswold example where land was worth 7s (35p) for farming, 6s (30p) for sport alone. Less intense cultivation meant better sport, as Jefferies pointed out in 'Nutty Autumn', *Nature Near London*

118 Crittall, *VCH Wilts*, IV, 371

119 Coulton, *Fourscore years*, 202

120 Jefferies, 'The Farmer's Parliament', *Hodge and His Masters* (1880)

121 Halèvy, *Imperialism and the Rise of Labour*, 295

122 Martin, *The Secret People*, 246 (quoting from *Transactions of the Devonshire Association*, 1922)

123 Robertson Scott, *England's Green and Pleasant Land*, 23

124 Thompson, *English Landed Society*, 303, quoting Jones, 'Land-owning as a Business', *Nineteenth Century* (1882), 346–68

125 Graham, *Rural Exodus* (1892), 16–17; and large prosperous tenant farmers, *RC2*, Q34515

126 Hence the papers by Price and Steele, *JRSS*, 55 and 67 (1892 and 1904); Price was Treasurer of Oriel College, Oxford

127 *RC2*, Q47433

128 Chadwick, *Victorian Church*, II, 367 and 168

129 Reeve, *Cambridge*, 117

130 *RC2*, Q30010, on the ruinous cost of grassing down arable

131 Perren, 'The Landlord and Agricultural Transformation', *AgHR*, 18 (1970), 36–51

132 Inheriting Savernake in 1894, the fifth Marquess of Aylesbury found an estate charged with jointures of £5,000 on a rental down from £38,000 in 1867 to £17,700 in 1896; Thompson, *English Landed Society*, 314

133 MacGregor, *History of Landownership*, 119 and 152

134 Perren, *AgHR*, 18 (1970), 36–51

135 Thompson, 'English Great Estates', *First Int Conf Econ Hist* (1960), 390–1

136 Between November 1879 and February 1880 the Inclosure Commissioners received applications for drainage money as great as their total drainage expenditure in 1876, 1877 or 1878. See *RC1*, Q4750, evidence of J. B. Denton, Engineer of the General Land Drainage and Improvement Co. The Director of a similar company observed that they had scarcely noticed the depression (Q2122–3)

137 Beastall, 'South Yorkshire Estate', *AgHR*, 14 (1966), 40–4, notes land purchase as characteristic of 1862–72, and disinclination to buy despite offers in 1872–99

138 Thompson, *JRSS*, 70 (1907), Table VII, 603

139 Dulac, *Agriculture et libre-échange*, 58–9

140 Thompson entitles the last chapter of *English Landed Society* thus

Chapter 4   Farmers in the Depression: Finance, Migration, and the Size of Farms

1 *WLC* gives figures for 1894: England 85 per cent, Wales 88

per cent, and Scotland 88 per cent (1896, XXXIV, 582). A surprisingly large number of *RC1* and *RC2* witnesses claimed to be
both landowners and tenant farmers

2   *RC1*, Q46093
3   *RC1*, Q45909
4   Perry, *AgHR*, 20 (1972), map 1
5   Compare Pringle, 'Report on Ongar, etc', *RC2* (1894), XVI, Pt 1,
    697–801, with the evidence of A. Darby (15 August 1895) and
    C. Matthews (8 November 1895)
6   *RC1*, Q51731
7   *RC2*, Q33724. See also Read, 'Large and small holdings', *JRASE*,
    2 (1887). 'Few farmers keep accurate accounts . . . small farmers
    never do.'
8   *RC2* (1894), XVI, Pt 2, 614–15
9   Gavin, 78 and 86
10 Summarised as Appendix 2, 348–55, of Channing, *The Truth
    about the Agricultural Depression* (1897)
11 Mentioned as an inducement to experienced men to return (*RC2*,
    Q36374) but much less often than falling rents, lower prices, and
    the generally depressed state of farming. Undercapitalisation was
    mentioned in the 1890s (*RC2*, Q61091 and 24382–3) but the latter
    (Scottish) witness's evidence indicates a 20 per cent reduction
    in capital needs
12 Bear, 'The Survival in farming', *JRASE*, 2 (1891), 270–1
13 Little, 'Report on Southern Counties', *RC1* (1881), XVI, 420,
    citing an estimate by the President of the Surveyors' Institute:
    RC1, Q4488
14 Wilson Fox, 'Cumberland', *RC2* (1895), XVII, 491
15 Bellerby and Boreham, 'Farm Occupiers' Capital in the United
    Kingdom before 1939', *Farm Economist*, 7 (1952–4), 257–63
16 Frequently mentioned before *RC2*, eg Q30278, 41182, 47966. As
    such witnesses pointed out, living off capital made it harder to
    leave, inhibited changes of system, and made the farm harder to
    let when it did become vacant
17 *RC2*, Q47474
18 Pringle, 'Bedfordshire, etc', *RC2* (1895), XVII, 18: one of the
    best examples of Pringle's ability and tendency to dramatise the
    situation
19 *RC1*, Q44612, Hope, a Scottish Assistant Comissioner
20 Brodrick, *English Land and English Landlords* (1881), 293
21 'The Fine Lady Farmer—Country Girls', *Hodge and His Masters*
22 Hall, *Pilgrimage of British Farming*, 214
23 *RC2*, Q3537 ; Druce, 'Report on Eastern Counties', *RC1* (1881),
    XVI, 376

24　Coleman, 'Report on Northern Counties', *RC1* (1881), XV1, 148 ; *RC2*, Q2077

25　Orr, *Oxfordshire*, 33

26　Orr, *Berkshire*, 19

27　Rew, 'Dorset', *RC2* (1895), XVII, 255

28　For newspapers used see bibliography (pp 186–7). For discussion, Perry and Johnston, 'Temporal and spatial incidence of agricultural depression', *Journal of Interdisciplinary History*, 3 (1972), 297–311

29　*RC2*, Q35677

30　*RC2*, Q8031. While this witness spoke of many changes, another from the county (*RC2*, Q4129) spoke of few ; the former refers to mid-Staffordshire, the latter to Needwood Forest in the east of the county

31　*RC1*, Q49527

32　*RC2*, Q43817

33　Coleman, 'Report on Northern Counties', *RC1* (1882), XV 652

34　Taylor, *Gillett's*, Chapter 10, notes rural emigration in 1887, and the presence of an 'emigration agent' in Banbury in 1890. References in *RC1* and *RC2* are numerous, eg *RC1*, Q36005 for the Lothians

35　*RC1*, Q50390, a witness from an inland county, Northamptonshire

36　*RC2*, Q60054, Cardiganshire. The jobs mentioned were connected with farming, namely dealing, auctioneer's clerk

37　Rew, 'Norfolk', *RC2* (1895), XVII, 359. It was estimated (Ibid) that 10 per cent of farmers in the East Dereham district were bankrupt, a commonplace use of loose terminology and round numbers

38　*RC2*, Q41182

39　*RC2*, Q8103

40　*RC2*, Q37656

41　*RC2*, Q9284

42　Speir, 'Ayr, etc', *RC2* (1895), XVII, 429 and 547

43　*RC2*, Q43750

44　Wrightson, 'Agricultural lessons of the "eighties" ', *JRASE*, 1 (1890), 276

45　*RC2*, Q36374 and 36508

46　*RC2*, Q52457

47　Fream, 'Andover and Maidstone', *RC2* (1894), XVI, Pt 1, 483

48　This section is based largely on Smith, E. L., *Go East for a Farm: a study of rural migration* (Oxford, 1932)

49　My colleague Dr. R. G. Cant comments that his farming forebears migrated from Scotland to Essex in the seventeenth century

50 Skeel, 'The cattle trade', *Trans Roy Hist Soc*, 9 (1926), 135–48

51 Walker, 'Report on Northern Scotland', *RC1* (1881), XVI, 549–60, cites the Kinross example, ironically more distant from Glasgow and climatically more severe than Lanarkshire ; land hunger was the prime factor

52 *WLC*, Q17048–51 (Breconshire) and 17542–45 where Welsh tenants had been evicted. *RC1*, Q451 describes Manx tenants as usually lowland Scots

53 Dorset Record Office, Estate Memoranda, Earl of Ilchester's Estates 1877 (uncatalogued), 90. The farm, at Somerton, drew twelve applicants ; others drew only local applicants, and some (undated) a single enquiry

54 Wilson Fox, 'Suffolk', *RC2* (1895), XVI, 376 ; most were from Ayrshire

55 Pringle, 'Ongar, etc', *RC2* (1894), XVI, Pt 1, 712. Pringle's view is more localised and for a shorter period. How far does Smith depend on Pringle?

56 Fream, 'Andover and Maidstone', *RC2* (1894), XVI, Pt 1, 483 ; Pringle, 'Bedford, etc', *RC2* (1895), XVII, 19–21, but 51–52 only partly supports this view

57 *RC1*, Q55733

58 *RC2*, Q48101 (Pringle)

59 *RC2*, Q34399. At this price demand was good according to the land-agent witness

60 Channing, *Truth about the Agricultural Depression* (1897), 10

61 Ingram, *VCH Sussex*, II, 286, in a district where the local preference was for annual tenancies

62 Ernle, 391 ; Orr, *Berkshire*, 57

63 McConnell, 'Experiences of a Scotsman', *JRASE*, 2 (1891), 323 ; but local stock were bought, too

64 Hall, *Pilgrimage of British Farming* (1913), 38

65 McConnell, 323–4

66 'Scottish farming in Essex', *Country Life*, 8 (1900), 396–8. The anonymous author, possibly McConnell, describes this as a traditional view of their success

67 Pringle, 'Ongar, etc', *RC2* (1894), XVI, Pt 1, 705–6, noted that even Scots came to use bare fallow. In his *RC2* evidence he observed that they found laying down permanent pasture difficult (Q11643)

68 Wilson Fox, 'Suffolk', *RC2* (1895), XVI, 705–6 and 712

69 *RC2*, Q61663, the comment of a successful Essex farmer

70 McGregor, *History of Landownership*, 134, notes that in 1894 one Cambridgeshire landowner spent £13 4s 5d (£13·22) on such advertising

71 Oxley Parker, 159
72 Oxley Parker, 161–2. In this case advertising was also pro-
    posed ; neither method succeeded. Although many English land-
    owners also had Scottish estates, I have come across no refer-
    ences to direct transfer
73 Does the *WLC* assertion (Q7722) that most failed reflect
    chauvinism and jealousy rather than reality? Likewise the assert-
    ion (53692–3) that they usually got leases in a land notorious
    for insecure tenures? Smith's observations on the Rugby district
    run counter to the older *WLC* view that language and religion
    inhibited Welsh farmer mobility (1896, XXXIV, 82–7)
74 Ernle, *The Pleasant Land of France* (1908) ; while Jefferies
    could admire the French peasant, he opposed subdivision,
    'Workers in the Wheat-fields' (no date), *Field and Hedgerow*
75 Venn, *Agricultural Economics*, 132
76 Clapham, *Economic History of Modern Britain*, II, 262–4 ; Venn,
    129
77 Price, 'The Commission on Agriculture', *EJ*, 6 (1896), 398
78 For subsistence standards of living see Jessopp, *Arcady* (1887),
    11 ; Wilson Fox, 'Cumberland', *RC2* (1895), XVII, 498
79 Pringle, 'Ongar, etc', *RC2* (1894), XVI, Pt 1, 731, notes the rise
    of poultry and small fruit farming in this depressed locality
    not far from London
80 Read, 'Large and small holdings', *JRASE*, 23 (1887), 27, ends
    his survey with a rhetorical question as to which can better
    survive hard times. Thompson, *VCH Wilts,* IV, 106, notes that
    large farmers survived better on the Wilton estates, in contrast
    to *RC2* assertions to the contrary (Q7245–6)
81 Pringle, 'Isle of Axholme', *RC2* (1894), XVI, Pt 1, 671–96, notably
    the most detailed of such reports
82 *WLC* (1896), XXXIV, 588 ; Wilson Fox, 'Cumberland', *RC2*
    (1895), XVII, 498
83 Thompson, 'English Great Estates', *First Int Conf Econ Hist*
    (1960), 393
84 *RC2*, Q630–1 and 13419–20, in the latter case to 120 acres
85 *RC2,* Q21025 ; Ruston and Witney, *Hooton Pagnell,* 192, although
    an increase in 5–20 acre holdings in the late 1880s is noted.
86 Orr, *Berkshire*, 19
87 Buckle, *VCH Dorset*, II, 276 ; Coleman, 'Report on Northern
    Counties', *RC1* (1881), XVI, 178
88 *RC1*, Q34325 (Lichfield), Q6716 (Yorkshire) ; higher rents and
    inadequate reserves are also mentioned. By contrast *RC2*,
    Q14874–6, suggests a widespread availability of small tenants
    with enough capital

89 Beastall, 'South Yorkshire Estate', *AgHR*, 14 (1966), 43. By contrast long-distance movement was generally from small to large farms, Smith, Chapter 3

90 Haggard, *Rural England* (1902), 274–8. It is of interest to note that over the years there has been a tendency to agglomeration, and only three smallholdings survive—personal communication from Miss Gillian Samways, Martinstown, Dorchester

91 Coleman, 'Report on Northern Counties', *RC1* (1881), XVI, 229–30. There is no similar reference to colliers

92 Beastall, 'South Yorkshire Estate', *AgHR*, 14 (1966), 42, notes that between 1862 and 1900 rents fell 6s 1d (30½p) on 300–400 acre farms, 1s 2d (6p) on 100–200 acre farms

93 *RC1*, Q61784

Chapter 5   Farmers in the Depression: The Practice of Farming

1 Astor and Rowntree, *British Agriculture*, 70
2 Gavin, *Ninety Years of Family Farming*, 76
3 Besse, *La crise et l'évolution de l'agriculture*, 104, suggests a fall in farm prices of 21·5 per cent between 1878 and 1888, and a fall in farm wages of 6·02 per cent during this period
4 *DAP* (1906), XCVI, 615
5 Jefferies, 'Weeds and Waste' (1878), *Chronicles of the Hedges*; Little, 'Report on Southern Counties', *RC1* (1881), XVI, 400, notes that grass was damaged as much or more than arable by adverse seasons
6 *DAP* (1906), XCVI, 633: 'The dykes lie in their tumbledown state faced with one or two lines of barbed wire'
7 Taylor, *Gillett's* (1964), 166, quotes the *Banbury Guardian* of 20 January 1880: 'The decrease in the number of hunters may to some extent be attributed to the agricultural depression, for it is a well known fact that with many lovers of the chase farming will not, to use a common phrase, "run to hunting" '
8 For example, Wilson Fox, 'Suffolk', *RC2* (1895), XVI, 378–9: 'They eat a good deal of porridge and brown bread, which Suffolk people would not touch'
9 Jessopp, *Arcady*, 11
10 Pringle, 'Isle of Axholme', *RC2* (1894), XVI, Pt 1, 681
11 *RC1*, Q7350
12 *A Century of Agricultural Statistics* (1968), passim, the basis of most discussion of this kind in this chapter
13 Long, *Handbook for Farmers* (1892), 5
14 As advocated and practised by Lord Leicester, for example;

Rew, 'Norfolk', *RC2* (1895), XVII, 373 ; Pringle (*RC2* Q8728) noted the possibilities of rotation grass in Essex. In these counties popular opinion on this matter was much more conservative, and even Pringle (eg *RC2*, Q8628) admitted the difficulties

15 Little, 'Report on Southern Counties', *RC1* (1882), XV, 63
16 Pringle, 'Ongar, etc', *RC2* (1894), XVI, Pt 1, 717–18, is probably the best known example
17 Prout, *Profitable Clay Farming* (1881), advocating cereal monoculture
18 Hall, *Pilgrimage of British Farming,* 17–18
19 Rowe, 'Cornish Agriculture', *Jnl Royal Inst Cornwall*, 3 (1957–60), 48
20 For example, Evans and Bowstead, 'Report on laying down land', *JRASE*, 11 (1875), 442–509, evidencing an interest in the matter before the depression ; Randell, 'Laying down clay land', *JRASE*, 18 (1882), 368–70
21 Witness the Duke of Bedford's experiences, discussed in *A Great Agricultural Estate,* 204–5
22 Randell believed that 3 years of limited sheep grazing, together with drainage and fertiliser, was the right start for new permanent grass—he knew that too often the reverse applied
23 For an example see Spencer, 'Vale of Aylesbury and Hertford', *RC2* (1895), XVI, 81. It took place nonetheless ; thus one-third of the Carse of Gowrie, strong land, went down between 1874 and 1894 (*RC2*, Q24408)
24 Rew, 'Norfolk', *RC2* (1895), XVII, 373
25 Franklin, *British Grasslands*, 132–6
26 *RC1*, Q48239 ; Orr, *Berkshire*, 57 ; Speir, 'Change in cropping to suit altered conditions of farming', *HAS*, 2 (1890), 65–78, enumerates several such approaches
27 Malden, 'Recent changes in farm practice', *JRASE*, 22 (1896), 22–38 makes this point ; likewise Hammond, *Livestock changes in Norfolk*, 8, for animals
28 Coppock, 'Agricultural changes in the Chilterns 1875–1900', *AgHR*, 9 (1961), 1–16
29 Thus Malden, note 27
30 Pringle, 'Ongar, etc', *RC2* (1894), XVI, Pt 1, 729–30 and 796–801 ; also his evidence (22 February and 9 March 1894)
31 *RC1*, Q61674. Essex Scots were among Sutton's growers by the 1890s. See *RC2*, Q17957
32 Hope, 'Roxburgh, etc', *RC2* (1895), XVII, 580
33 Thirsk, *English peasant farming: the agrarian history of Lincolnshire,* 315
34 *RC2*, Q8053

35 Ingram, *VCH Sussex*, II 275, cites grassing down for dairying in the Weald; for letting farms see, for example, *RC1*, Q55579, and statements in advertisements of farms to let such as 'the quality of arable land can be reduced if desired by an incoming tenant' (West Lydford, Somerset, 1894)

36 Hope, 'Perth, etc', *RC2* (1894), XVI, Pt 1, 819, with respect to Aberdeenshire

37 For example, Bear, 'Our agricultural population', *EJ*, 4 (1894), 317–31

38 Duke of Bedford, 195

39 *DAP* (1906), XCVI, 593

40 Ibid, 690

41 Rew, 'Dorset', *RC2* (1895), XVII, 256

42 *RC2*, Q8688

43 Besse, 93

44 *DAP* (1906), XCVI, 688 and 692

45 Stevens, *Sheep*, Pt 2, 30, for the change from mutton to lamb; Burnett, *Plenty and Want,* 180, for upper-class tastes

46 Trow-Smith, *British Livestock Husbandry*, 303

47 Coppock, *Agricultural Atlas of England and Wales* (1964), 180

48 Hammond, *Livestock Changes in Norfolk*, 8

49 Rew, 'Salisbury Plain', *RC2* (1895), XVI, 492

50 Spencer, 'Vale of Aylesbury and Hertford', *RC2* (1895), XVI, 81

51 Elwes and Malden, 'Cross-bred sheep', *JRASE*, 6 (1895), 222–5

52 Hutcheson, 'Past and future of Scottish agriculture', *HAS*, 11 (1899), 127

53 Harvey, *History of Farm Buildings,* 186

54 Grigg, 'Development of tenant right in South Lincolnshire', *Lincs Historian*, 2 (1962), 41–7, notes that no allowance was made for grassing down; for Scotland, see Walker, 'Report on Northern Scotland', *RC1* (1881), XVI, 565–6

55 Orr, *Berkshire*, 13–14

56 *RC1*, Q51404–5; neither could the estate be charged nor could the land improvement and drainage companies lend for this purpose

57 Rew, 'Norfolk', *RC2* (1895), XVII, 344

58 Franklin, *British Grasslands*, 136–7

59 Youatt, *Complete Grazier* (1893), 1013; WLC (1896), XXXIV, 771

60 Wilson Fox, 'Cumberland', *RC2* (1895), XVII, 496

61 Pringle, 'Ongar, etc', *RC2* (1894), XVI, Pt 1, 723–4

62 Discussed in Whetham, 'London milk trade', *EcHR*, 17 (1964), 369–80

63 McConnell, *JRASE*, 2 (1891), 311–12, gave low rents as a reason for moving to Essex; S. W. Farmer's dairy enterprise around Pewsey began on empty farms, Thompson, *VCH Wilts*, IV, 106–7

64 The Essex Scots are the best known and documented example. Hall, 161-2, notes the integration of dairying into the existing arable system in Wiltshire

65 Fletcher, 'Lancashire Livestock Farming', *AgHR*, 9 (1961), 26–7, implies no fall in price. Other areas were less favoured; Spencer, 'Vale of Aylesbury and Hertford', *RC2* (1895), XVI, 95, suggests a fall from 6s 11d (34·5p) to 5s 10d (29p) per gallon in Aylesbury between 1884 and 1893

66 Druce, 'Report on Eastern Counties', *RC1* (1882), XV, 274

67 Fussell, 'Four centuries of farming systems in Derbyshire', *Jnl Derbys A and NH Soc*, 71 (1951)

68 Besse, 145

69 Hall, 404, referring to south-west Scotland

70 Ashworth, *Economic History of England* (1960), 47

71 Little, 'Report on Southern Counties', *RC1* (1881), XVI, 428

72 Besse, 142, gives values of 1s 6d to 1s 10d) (7·5p to 9p) for fresh milk, and 10d to 1s (4p to 5p) for its butter equivalent

73 Butter was first shipped to Britain from New Zealand in 1882, and by 1903 250,000cwt was shipped annually

74 Garnett, *Westmoreland*, 139–40, gives a peak butter price of 2s to 2s 2d (10–11p) in 1874–5 compared with 11½d (almost 5p) in 1897; Ralston, 'Wigtownshire', *HAS*, 1 (1885), 130, gives even more catastrophic figures for cheese in the late 1870s, from 64s–68s (£3·20–£3·40) to 36s–40s (£1·80 to £2). More general surveys give lower estimates; *RC2* (1897), XV, 43–53, gives 25–33 per cent for dairy products 1874–91, and 16 per cent for butter 1876–8 to 1892–4

75 Jefferies, 'Haymaking—"The Juke's Country"', *Hodge and His Masters,* related low cheese prices to depression in the iron trade. Canadian and US imports were the real culprits (*RC1*, Q1836 and 3758)

76 *RC1*, Q48749

77 *RC1*, Q34001 (Frocester, Glos), Q34383 (Staffordshire)

78 *RC1*, Q57413. In Derbyshire prices rose from 64s (£3·20) in 1878 to 80s (£4) in 1880, the highest since 1873–4

79 Besse, 385; Astor and Rowntree, 66

80 Burnett, 107

81 *RC1*, Q55996, a Yorkshire farm on Lord Leconfield's estate

82 'Scottish farming in Essex', *Country Life*, 8 (1900), 396–8

83 Thompson, *VCH Wilts,* IV, 106. Ironically landlord intransigence over rents precipitated the situation

84 Hall, 412–13, discusses extensive production in the Midlands; Thirsk and Imray, 'Suffolk farming in the nineteenth century', *Suffolk Record Society*, 1 (1958), 36, mentions a form of zero-grazing with Ayrshire cows fed on hot food and brewers' grains

85 Gavin, *Ninety Years of Family Farming*, Chapter 7. The retail outlet, Lord Rayleigh's Dairies, was set up in 1900

86 Kendall, *Farming Memoirs of a West Country Yeoman,* 17

87 Gavin, Chapter 10

88 Fussell, 'Cornish Farming', *Amateur Historian*, 4 (1960), 345

89 McConnell, 'Experiences of a Scotsman', *JRASE*, 2 (1891), 323–4

90 *RC2*, Q8909 and 3476; Wilson Fox, 'Garstang', *RC2* (1894), XVI, Pt 1, 557; Thirsk, *VCH Leics*, II, 951

91 Coppock, 'Agricultural change in the Chilterns', *AgHR*, 9 (1961), 12

92 McConnell, 322

93 Fussell, 'Glamorgan Farming', *Morgannwg*, 1 (1957), 41

94 Fussell, *English Dairy Farmer*, 220, notes that the Bath and West offered dairy courses from 1888, the first year in which the Royal Show gave butter prizes

95 Hall, 117-18

96 *RC1*, Q51189

97 Trow-Smith, *British Livestock Husbandry 1700–1900*, 306–7

98 Fussell, *English Dairy Farmer*, 55

99 Thompson, *VCH Wilts*, IV, 102

100 Rew, 'Heathfield', *RC2* (1895), XVI, 450

101 Sayers, *Economic change in England* (1967), 111. Examples of original hand-barbed wire are still in use in New Zealand, but I know of no British examples

102 Fussell, *English Dairy Farmer*, 318. How many rustic hernias were caused by the 17-gallon churns then in use? This amount of milk weighs about 170lb (75kg)

103 Ibid, 314–15 and 319

104 *RC1*, Q1822

105 *RC2*, Q5131

106 For buildings, see Wilson Fox, 'Garstang', *RC2* (1894), XVI, Pt 1, 559–60. Financial problems are stressed in G. Lambert's 'Minority Report', *RC2* (1897), XV, 206

107 Smith, *Go East for a Farm*, Chapter 4, suggests that even Scottish migrants felt thus, but were too shrewd to be ruled by their feelings. A. G. Street's novel *Farmer's Glory* (1932) expresses this dilemma as felt in the renewed depression of the 1920s

108 Venn, *Agricultural Economics*, 12–13

109 Gavin, 86

110 *RC2*, Q8909 (Pringle, noting that such success depended on command of adequate capital)

111 Chaplin, 'Supplementary Memorandum', *RC1* (1882), XIV, 38

112 *FI* (1905), XX, 546

113 Caird, *Landed Interest and Supply of Food*, 174–5

114 *FI* (1905), XX, 546–7

115 In *RC1*, Q51096, a Kent witness gave foreign competition as a reason why orchards were not being extended, but *FI* (1905), XX, 571, advances the counter-argument of creation of a public taste

116 For example housing in Essex, *RC2*, Q34447

117 Fruit and potato crops were badly affected in Huntingdonshire in 1879. See Druce, 'Report on Eastern Counties', *RC1* (1881), XVI, 369

118 Beavington, 'Early market gardening', *IBG*, 37 (1965), dates growth at Sandy from 1851; Pratt, *Transition in Agriculture*, Chapter 11, discusses Evesham

119 *FI* (1906), XXIV, 432; Little, 'Report on Southern Counties', *RC1* (1882), XV, 25

120 Ernle, 391; Eagle, 'Lincolnshire bulb industry', *Lincs Historian*, 6 (1950), 220–9; Pratt, Chapter 4; Thirsk, *English peasant farming . . . Lincolnshire*, 315–16

121 Graham, *Revival of English Agriculture* (1899), 213, and *Rural Exodus* (1892), 159

122 Eagle, 229

123 Graham, *Revival*, 202

124 *RC1*, Q56451—probably the Maidstone district. Nevertheless the acreage was growing (Q56446)

125 *RC1*, Q55336

126 Little, 'Report on Southern Counties', *RC1* (1882), XV, 50

127 Discussed by *FI* (1905), XX, 15

128 Ibid, 13–14

129 Pratt, *Transition*, 130–2

130 *FI* (1906), XXIV, Tables 2 and 4, 432–3 and 435–6

131 Venn, 132

132 Rew, near Dorchester is probably a good example. See Chapter 4, note 90

133 Graham, *Rural Exodus*, Chapter 3, notes the success of townsmen in the Fens, where labourers (lacking suitable skills and capital) left the district. Eagle notes the role of businessmen's initiative at Spalding

134 Spencer, *VCH Surrey*, IV, 463, notes such developments around Guildford

135 Rew, 'Heathfield', *RC2* (1895), XVI, 445–76. Climate was still

important in this matter, *RC1*, Q54649, according, surprisingly, to a Putney witness

136 *RC1*, Q51417 and 51486: 'There is care taken with little things . . . men are making a living where other men would starve'

137 Jefferies, 'A Lesson in Lent' (1877), *Chronicles of the Hedges*. The *Dorset County Chronicle* (26 August 1880) carried an advertisement seeking to rent a 300 acre farm to turn into a warren.

138 Graham, *Rural Exodus*, 153

139 As early as 1878 Smyth (*HAS*, 10 [1878], 255–75) could demonstrate that forestry was the most profitable use of poor land

140 Long, *Handbook for Farmers* (1892), 129–30

141 *RC1*, Q45307: 'We must endeavour to reduce our expenditure, to adopt a higher system of farming, to be more liberal with our manures, to approach more nearly, if possible, gardening'. Q45428 picks up the inconsistency of this position

142 *RC1*, Q4684, suggests that less attention was given to this matter than 20 years previously ; Walker, *Farming to Profit* (1888), and Prout, *Profitable Clay Farming* (1881), say little of horticulture

143 Brodrick, *English Land and English Landlords* (1881), 296

144 Fussell, 'Four centuries of farming systems in Shropshire', *Trans Salop Arch Soc,* 54 (1953), 1–29

145 Walker, *Farming to Profit* (1888), 2 ; *RC1*, Q36174 (Lothians)

146 *RC1*, Q53030

147 Venn, Tables 5 and 6, 555–6, based on Lawes and Gilbert, *JRASE*, 16 (1880), and official statistics (Fig 7, p 38)

148 Channing, *Truth about the Agricultural Depression*, 30–37

149 Hutcheson, 'The past and future of Scottish agriculture', *HAS*, 11 (1899), 124

150 McConnell, *JRASE*, 2 (1891), 320

151 Channing, 'Minority report', *RC2* (1897), XV, 253–4

152 Gavin, 86

153 Ditchfield and Simmons, *VCH Berks*, II, 337

154 Coleman, 'Report on Northern Counties', *RC1* (1881), XVI, 145

Chapter 6   Labourers and Legislators

1 There were 983,919 agricultural labourers and farm servants in Britain in 1881 (shepherds excluded), and 689,292 in 1901 (shepherds excluded). Farmers and graziers at these dates numbered 279,126 and 277,694 respectively. *DAP* (1906), XCVI, 699 and 698

2   Jones and Pool, *Hundred Years of Economic Development*, 222–5, suggests that if 1880=100, 1900=140

3   Burnett, *Plenty and Want*, 92

4   Burnett, 115, quoting Canon Girdlestone, the north Devon radical who organised migration schemes from his overpopulated rural parish

5   Burnett, 135: 'Underfeeding was still the lot of the majority of labourers in 1914'.

6   The minimum acceptable height for recruits in 1900 was 5 ft

7   Rowntree, *How the labourer lives* (1913), 328–31

8   Rowntree, 315 et seq

9   *RC1*, Q65274 (Axholme), and in many other sources and localities

10 Dunbabin, 'The incidence and organisation of agricultural trades unionism in the 1870s', *AgHR*, 16 (1968), 114–41

11 Sauerbeck's index was at 100 in 1875, 65 in 1899; Layton and Crowther, *Study of Prices*, 230–1

12 Rowntree, 20, claims that 9,000 farm workers emigrated in 1900, and 33,000 (about 1 in 40) in 1911

13 *RC2* (1894), XVI, Pt 1, 619, Table VII

14 For example, *RC1*, Q33364. Kendall's failure to comment (*Farming Memoirs of a West Country Yeoman*) until after 1900 may therefore be significant

15 Dulac gives values for wages as (a) 55 per cent of net profit in 1875–81, and 120 per cent in 1889–95; and (b) 35 per cent of production in 1875–81 and 55 per cent in 1889–95. See also *RC2*, Q16325–6

16 Hardy, 'The Dorsetshire Labourer', *Longmans Magazine*, 2 (1883), 264. Arch appeared before *RC1* on 4 August 1881

17 'Scottish farming in Essex', *Country Life*, 8 (1900), 396–8, ascribes success to low living standards. But, as Smith, Chapter 3, points out, movement was characteristically from family labour to wage labour districts. McConnell, for example, had no family labour

18 *DAP* (1906), XCVI, 621 (Glos)

19 *RC2*, Q34597

20 *RC2*, Q2100

21 Bedfordshire Record Office, R. W. Foll's labour account on Chalgrave Manor Farm 1875–1906, X52/71

22 Evans, *Where Beards Wag All*, 252

23 Partridge, *Early Agricultural Machinery*, 14, states that the first binder was exhibited in 1876; Clapham, *Economic History of Modern Britain*, III, 89–90, believed them to be important in labour economy. Sayers, *History of Economic Change*, III, claims complete success by the mid-1880s

24 Wilkinson, 'Summary report,' *RCL* (1893–4), XXXV, 736
25 Smith, *No Rain in These Clouds,* 53 and 57
26 Perry, 'Working class isolation and mobility in rural Dorset, 1837–1936: a study of marriage distances', *IBG*, 46 (1969), 121–42, demonstrates that personal mobility greatly increased between the decades 1877–86 and 1887–96. See also *RC2*, Q55398 (Berwickshire)
27 Rowntree, 323
28 *RC1*, Q50952
29 Roxby, 'Rural depopulation', *Nineteenth Century*, 431 (1912), 174–90 ; Ashby, *Joseph Ashby of Tysoe*, 149–50
30 Richards, 'District Report—Bromyard', *RCL* (1893–4), XXXV, 569
31 Druce, 'The alteration in the distribution of the agricultural population', *JRASE*, 21 (1885), 108–10
32 Bear, 'Our agricultural population', *EJ*, 4 (1894), 3
33 'Scottish farming in Essex', *Country Life*, 8 (1900), 396–8 ; Graham, *Revival of English agriculture* (1899), 263
34 Graham
35 Chapman, 'District Report—Thame', *RCL* (1893–4), XXXV, 206 ; Wilson Fox, 'District Report—Wigton (Cumberland)', *RCL* (1893–4), XXXV, 459: 'A good many men were not hired this November (1892) owing to agricultural depression'
36 Green, *English Agricultural Labourer* (1920), 76, 110, comments on the adverse effects of bad weather ; *RC1*, Q46538, claims that wet and late harvests cancelled out attempts at labour economy in the East Riding
37 Jessopp, *Arcady*, 117
38 Evans, *Where Beards Wag All,* 250. The career of Ernest Bevin exemplifies the possibilities open to the country boy working with horses in the city
39 Especially the shortage of skilled men, eg Wilkinson, 'District Report—Easingwold', *RCL* (1893–4), XXXV, 795
40 Ojala, *Agriculture and Economic Progress*, 133, Table 55
41 Jefferies, 'Midsummer' (1879), *Chronicles of the Hedges*: 'The general depression of agriculture and the price of labour has . . . led farmers to stint expenditure on labour, so that the cleaning of soil has not well been carried out. Now the consequences of this neglect—in many cases forced upon them—are apparent: the weeds are rampant'
42 McConnell, 'Experiences of a Scotsman', *JRASE*, 2 (1891), 317–19
43 Hunt, 'Labour productivity in English agriculture', *EcHR*, 20 (1967), 285–8
44 Dulac, *Agriculture et libre-échange,* 45

45 Hunt, 292

46 Bear, 'Our agricultural population', *EJ*, 4 (1894), 317–31, finds no evidence of dullness as a factor in rural depopulation. Contemporary newspapers and grandparental reminiscence support Bear. King and Arch, 'Statistics of some Midland villages', *EJ*, 3 (1893), 22, comments on the varying level of social activity from village to village

47 For example, *RC1*, Q40967 (Lothians), favours free trade, and Druce, 'Report on Eastern Counties', *RC1* (1882), XV, 350, believed only a minority favoured protection ; but *RC1*, Q66971 (Bentinck, MP for West Norfolk), advocates protection

48 McDowell, *British Conservatism 1832–1914*, 153

49 McDowell, 153 et seq

50 Little, 'Report on Southern Counties', *RC1* (1881), XVI, 424–5. Nearby at Faringdon 'protection was out of the question'

51 Druce (see note 47) ; Doyle, 'Report on Midland Counties', *RC1* (1881), XVI, 281

52 For example, Turner, 'Stratford upon Avon', *RC2* (1894), XVI, Pt 1, 578, under the euphemism of 'fair trade'

53 *RC2*, Q13876

54 At 3d (1·25p) per cwt on corn, 5d (2p) on flour, the duty was no more than a revival of Peel's nominal 1846 duties. Nevertheless it raised a political storm, and lost the Conservatives a by-election at Bury. See Halèvy, V, 321 and 329

55 Clapham, *Economic History of Modern Britain*, III, 76

56 For details see bibliography, pp 185–6

57 Gibb, *Fifty years in Lauderdale*, 131 ; Fletcher, 'Great depression' *EcHR*, 13 (1960–1), 417–32

58 *RC2*, Q24730

59 The Richmond Commission spent 9 days in Dublin in June 1880, and 27 days in London on Irish evidence ; Scottish evidence was heard in April and May 1881

60 'Supplementary Report' and 'Report of Chairman etc', *RC2* (1896), XVI, 433–4 and 434–43. See also *The Times*, parliamentary debates and correspondence (April–May 1896)

61 Fletcher, 'The Great Depression of English Agriculture', *EcHR*, 13 (1960–1), 430

62 Channing, 'Minority Report', *RC2* (1897), XV, 225–370

63 Everett, 'Memorandum', *RC2* (1896), XVI, 185–203

64 *RC2* (1896), XVI, 419

65 Doyle, who covered the Midlands for *RC1*, was probably the least expert, a former Poor Law inspector who knew 'nothing practically of farming' (Q32168, his own admission) ; his professional background emerges in his oral evidence (9–11 March

1881). A prominent defect of his report is its neglect of dairy-ing. Little and Hope of the *RC1* assistants were practical farmers, and among the *RC2* assistants Fream was the author of a very successful agricultural textbook

66 A prime area of dispute between Shaw-Lefevre and Chaplin. The Act was known as the Agricultural Rating Act 1896

67 Chaplin was its President from 1889 to 1892, Ernle from 1916 to 1919. Chaplin regarded Ernle as rather weak in his role as a defender of agricultural interests

68 So called because it originated as a duty on spirits to pay com-pensation for the licences of redundant beerhouses. The re-dundancy measure was never carried, but the tax was diverted to the County Councils for this end; Ensor, *England 1870–1914*, 204 fn

69 In fact landowners and farmers remain prominent in the local government, and to a lesser degree the magistracy, of most rural counties in the 1970s

70 Thompson, 'Land Market in the Nineteenth Century', *Oxford Econ Papers*, 9 (1957), 303–4, notes that by protecting the capital sum rather than the land itself the Act facilitated sales and was thus in some respects pro-landlord. Some sales followed, but more generally the late nineteenth-century land market was thin and weak

71 Matthews, *Fifty Years of agricultural politics* (1915) is an in-valuable history of the Central Chamber. Ironically the word 'depression' does not appear in the index

72 'Final report', *RC2* (1896), XVI, 158

73 Dulac, *Agriculture et libre-échange*, ix

74 Clark, *The Making of Victorian England*, 240

75 Lloyd, *General Election of 1880*, 59–62 and 150

76 Gladstone, *Midlothian Speeches*, 96–114

77 For example, *Peterborough Advertiser* (6 September 1879)

78 Thompson, 'Land and politics in England', *Trans Roy Hist Soc*, 15 (1965), 23–44

79 Clark, 216

Chapter 7   Conclusion

1 Smith, *No Rain in These Clouds*, 21–5

2 Fletcher, 'The Great Depression,' *EcHR*, 13, (1960–1), 423

3 Rew, *Agricultural Faggot*, 36

4   Firey, *Man, Mind and Land*, 129–30
5   Wolpert, 'The decision process in a spatial context', *Annals of the Association of American Geographers*, 54 (1964), 558
6   Hall, *Pilgrimage of British farming*, 327
7   Thompson, 'The second agricultural revolution', *EcHR*, 21 (1968), 66
8   Martin, *The shearers and the shorn*, 103, quoting H. T. Gerrans, Assistant Commissioner, *Royal Commission on Secondary Education,* 1895. See also Thompson, 'English Great Estates', *First Int Conf Econ Hist* (1960), 397
9   Thompson, 390–4
10 Beales, ' "The Great Depression" in industry and trade', *EcHR*, 5 (1934), 74 fn
11 Wilson, 'Economy and Society in late Victorian Britain', *EcHR,* 18 (1965), 198
12 Rosenberg, 'Political and social consequences of the great depression of 1873–96', *EcHR*, 13 (1943), 58–73
13 *RC1*, Q1195
14 Clapham, *Economic History of Modern Britain*, III, 119
15 Astor and Rowntree, *British Agriculture*, 64
16 For example, the Mortgagors and Tenants Relief Act 1931 and the Rural Mortgagors Final Adjustment Act 1935 avowedly aiming to reduce rural indebtedness and write off excessive capitalisation
17 *WLC* (1896), XXXIV, 907
18 Burke, *Reflections on the Revolution in France*

Historiography and Bibliography

A COMPLETE AND exhaustive bibliography of this topic is a practical impossibility. Every newspaper and every agricultural journal of the period covers the field; passing, and often illuminating, references to the state of farming are commonplaces of contemporary novels and biography; record offices, estate archives, public and private libraries abound with the raw materials for a study of the depression. This bibliography discusses and lists, under a small number of broad headings, the materials used in writing this book.

The Royal Commissions have been discussed in a political context in Chapter 6. It remains to examine their relationship, as sources, to the totality and reality of the depression. This is less a problem with regard to the civil servants and landowners among its witnesses than with respect to farmers, merchants, and the few farm workers who gave evidence. These latter groups are unlikely to have been typical of their kind: almost certainly they were the keen and enthusiastic, the able and intelligent, and in this particular context the unfortunate and the unsuccessful; they were no random sample of grass-roots farming opinion. The itinerant Assistant Commissioners were better placed for this task: they were able to meet more farmers in less formal circumstances, including many who probably would not spontaneously have presented themselves; they collected and presented abundant statistical material. They were not without limitations, however (see Chapter 6, ref 65). The problems of the statistical material are those of the size of the undertaking and the necessarily diverse personnel employed. Even these dedicated men were not afraid to doubt the reality of the phenomenon they were commissioned to investigate in some areas.

Official records extend beyond commissions and committees of enquiry. Agricultural statistics at the parish level were collected from 1866, and may be regarded as reliable from the mid-1870s; the *London Gazette* published corn prices from a number of markets and, less known but in times of depression equally useful, lists and advertisements relating to bankruptcy. The problem remains that of understanding the relationship between so small and uncontrolled a sample and the total reality of which it is part, bankruptcy excepted.

The second major source to be considered is the press, more particularly the country newspapers, their news columns and their advertisements. These allow widespread attainment of uniformity and objectivity in the scholar's methods, and the attainment of a high degree of detail in investigating certain topics; but bulk, and thus time, pose literally forbidding problems for more than local study. For a few national weeklies this constraint is less serious, but so is the breadth and detail of treatment more limited. Of course not all newspapers were detailed and impartial—most were politically partisan and obviously so. They are at times tediously repetitive and at times naïve, but they also contain some of the finest writing on the depression—much of Richard Jefferies' early work in the *Wiltshire and Gloucestershire Standard* and *North Wiltshire Herald*, for example. Too often scholars have concentrated on such writing, and on news and editorial material, which suffer from defects similar to those of much official material. Too little work has been based on the austere and superficially undramatic advertisement columns, which provide a continuous and comparable flow of information on buying and selling, and on such matters as land sales, farm sales, and farms to let, all of which were important parameters of the depression.

There is no shortage of contemporary literature on the depression. The Victorian countryman was a voracious reader and writer: agricultural journalists were numerous, and particularly useful are the reflective and considered reminiscences of not a few farmers on the depression later in life.

Landowners, parsons, and more or less well informed outsiders ventured into print, in books, in such heavyweight journals as *Nineteenth Century* and the *Contemporary Review*, and in the agricultural press. At times farming appears to have been everyone's business, and thus nonsense as well as good sense appeared in print. How close a relationship this mass of material bears to the circumstances of the average farmer, the man on the agricultural omnibus, remains as real a problem as with much official and newspaper material. The typical 'Farmer Giles' appears in both didactic and reminiscent writings at secondhand, but it is the thoughts, actions, and aspirations of the able and ambitious which dominate the literary material.

Finally a mass of private papers rests in County Record Offices, university archives, estate offices and private houses over the length and breadth of Britain. Only a small proportion relates directly to farm worker or farmer; the latter rarely kept accounts at this date and even more rarely have they been preserved. But like the equally infrequently encountered farm diary these sources are of considerable importance. The most abundant, and among scholars the most favoured, source of this kind is the estate archive, for almost all landed properties kept records and most tried to improve whatever system, if any, they followed. Most estates kept some of their papers, but not always consistently or regularly; and estate archives sometimes fade out in the early years of the depression, perhaps as a result of it. Bulk and comparability are again problems, particularly for the more than local study, but the range of topics covered, such as rents, the selection of tenants, and investment policy, is attractively broad if often frustratingly fragmentary.

There is no scarcity of raw materials on which to build a study of the depression; there are obvious and less than obvious lacunae and shortcomings, however, and it is not possible for one scholar to look at all the sources. But if a start must be made in a state of incomplete understanding, it is important to understand the character of that imperfection, to be aware of the limitations of the materials, and to avoid excessive dependence on even the most attractive. Most writers have erred in the direction of either regarding the words of a handful of

writers and witnesses as trustworthy in a wide spatial and
temporal context, or they have disregarded all material other
than the seemingly most objective and dispassionate statistics.
The choice is one between flesh and bones: my aim has been
'to keep the mean between the two extremes, of too much
stiffness in refusing, and of too much easiness in admitting'.

HISTORIOGRAPHY

Among the many contemporary writers on the depression only
one may be regarded as a historian; the rest played the roles of
journalist, teacher, and not infrequently polemicist. In 1885
R. E. Prothero (later Lord Ernle), an Oxford-educated literary
journalist, was moved by evident agricultural distress to write
an essay called 'The pioneers and prospect of English agriculture' for the *Quarterly Review.* The essay set its author on
an agricultural course which led to the post of agent-in-chief
to the Duke of Bedford, President of the Board of Agriculture,
and the peerage; the final version of his essay appeared in
book form in 1912 as *English Farming Past and Present.* Later
editions, the most recent in 1961, have received considerable
revision, notably by Sir Daniel Hall in the latter part of the
chapter dealing with the depression. He wrote at no great
length on the depression, relying mainly on official sources and
personal observation and emphasising its more dismal aspects.
Dependence on a narrow range of sources, some inclination to
dramatisation and exaggeration, a failure to discuss the geography of the depression adequately, and above all his own
choice of a brief to defend the landed interest, are the weak-
nesses of a most influential piece of writing. As a recent critic
has warned, it must be 'read as a partisan contribution to the
late-nineteenth and early-twentieth century debate on the
function of the land in English society'. But until recently
Ernle's attractive work had no rivals, and its views were, therefore, those received and accepted by most non-specialist historians and interested laymen.

    Writing during the depression Ernle was nevertheless con-
cerned with a much broader canvas. Other writers have taken
a similar though less-extended position, eg Orwin and Whetham, and Astor and Rowntree. The only full-scale treatments

of the topic in its own right derive from French doctoral theses by Besse and Dulac written during the recovery phase following the depression. These theses are no formal rejection of Ernle's point of view; rather they are a less partisan development of it, with all the defects usually associated with doctoral dissertations. They evidence a continental interest in the willingness of the British to sacrifice their agriculture which reciprocates contemporary British interest in the apparent prosperity of European farmers. In fact many European countries and the eastern USA shared the British experience of adversity.

The best known critic and revisionist of Ernle's view is T. W. Fletcher, in two brief but brilliant articles in the *Economic History Review* and the *Agricultural History Review* in 1961. Fletcher believed that Ernle had paid too much attention to arable farming and grain prices, thus reflecting contemporary officialdom. Saul and Wilson, in discussing and criticising the view that the last quarter of the nineteenth century witnessed general economic depression, have accepted and developed Fletcher's position. But all, and Fletcher in particular, are selective of evidence—Fletcher leans heavily on the two *Royal Commissions*, on the *Economist*, and on newspaper evidence from Lancashire, a relatively unscathed county—and neglect a fact which Ernle could not fail to grasp, that many farmers and landowners from all over Britain believed they were experiencing hard times whatever the objective reality of their position.

This latter point has been taken up more by economists and geographers, attempting to measure and map the depression's incidence and to build spatial models, than by historians. Such studies, the earliest by Olson and Harris in 1959, are necessarily less than comprehensive, focused as they are on a single topic or locality, but they indicate the possibility of applying the techniques of the 'new' history and the 'new' geography. Other scholars have chosen different areas of concentration and less radical methods—for instance, Fussell and Whetham dairying, and Coppock land use and the Chilterns. This last approach, regionally, or even more locally through the medium of the estate archive, is the most prevalent of all. In some ways it is an evasion of difficult problems, and as with other methods the character of the sources used strongly affects the end product; but for all its inherent limitations such work is essential and illuminating, a good example being that of Beastall and Perren. Lastly there are useful discussions in books primarily concerned with other topics, such as Venn on the role of monetary factors, an interesting topic neglected by most other writers except Conacher.

In brief a corpus of older and newer scholarship discusses various aspects of the depression and what happened in various localities and according to various sources. Recent workers have challenged older views, but none have chosen to provide a detailed exposition. There is, of course, a perennial argument against such endeavour, best expressed in Thompson's words on the advisability of waiting 'until in some more perfect world sufficient evidence (and I would add scholarship) will have been accumulated to allow a committee of experts to compose *the* general history'. In other words the time is not ripe; but time 'is like the medlar; it has a trick of going rotten before it is ripe'. And excellent works have been written prematurely and precipitately, Clark's classic *Invasion of New Zealand by People, Plants and Animals* being one example. There is no doubt that the topic itself merits discussion in depth, and three or four generations of scholars have provided a substantial if incomplete body of work to serve as the basis for such discussion.

SELECT BIBLIOGRAPHY

British Parliamentary Papers (*BPP*) (Readex Microprint Edition)
A study of the depression necessarily begins with the two Royal Commissions. The *Royal Commission on the Depressed Condition of Agricultural Interests* (the Richmond Commission, *RC1*, 1880–82) produced the following papers (referred to as in the official *BPP* index for the years 1852–99, an indispensable volume, which appeared in 1909):
Preliminary Report (1881), XV, 1.
Final Report (1882), XIV, 1.
Minutes of Evidence: (1881), XV, 25; (1881), XVII, 1; (1882), XIV, 45.
Digest of Evidence: (1881), XVI, 1; (1882), XIV, 493.

Appendices: (1881), XVI, 1; (1882), XIV, 493.

Assistant Commissioners' Reports: (1880), XVIII, 1; (1881), XVI, 1, and 841; (1882), XV, 1. These cover the whole of Britain, Ireland, North America, parts of Europe, and specialised topics such as smallholdings. They are listed on p 785 of the official index. The most useful are by Little on the south and west (1881), XVI, 395 and (1882), XV, 1; and Druce on the east (1881), XVI, 363 and (1882), XV, 247.

The *Royal Commission on the Agricultural Depression* (*RC2*, 1894–7), produced the following papers:

First General Report (1894), XVI, Pts 1 to 3.

Second General Report (1896), XVI, 413.

Final General Report (1897), XV, 1.

Evidence and Appendices (1894), XVI, Pts 1 to 3.

Further Evidence and Appendices (1896), XVII, 1.

Appendices (1897), XV, 385.

Expenditure and outgoings on certain estates in Great Britain; and Farm Accounts (1896), XVI, 469.

Reports of Assistant Commissioners (1894), XVI, Pt 1, 471; (1895), XVI, 1; (1895), XVII, 1. These reports, unlike those of *RC1*, are not geographically comprehensive; they vary in scope from small areas to several counties. They are listed on p 20 of the official index.

The *Royal Commission on Land* (*Wales and Monmouthshire*) (the Welsh Land Commission, *WLC*, 1894–6) lacked nothing in fluency:

First Report (1894), XXVI, 1.

Second Report (1896), XXXIV, 1.

Evidence and Appendices (1894), XXXVI, 9; (1894), XXXVII, 1; (1895), XL, 1; (1895), XLI, 1; (1896) XXXV, 1; (1896), XXXIII, 555.

Index (1896), XXXV, 1.

The *Royal Commission on Labour* (*RCL*, 1892–4).

Assistant Commissioners' Reports on Agricultural Labourers (1893–4), XXXV, 1; (1893–4), XXXVI, 1; (1893–4), XXXVII, 1.

Evidence before Group B (Agriculture, etc) (1892), XXXV, 1; (1892), XXXVI, Pt 1, 5; (1893–4), XXXII, 5.

(See also official index, p 776.)

M

The *Report of the Select Committee on Corn Sale* (1890–94). Reports with evidence: (1890–91), XII, 192; (1892), XI, 5; (1893–4), XI, 1 (with index). Concerned mainly with technical aspects of buying and selling, eg weights and measures.
Departmental Committee of the Board of Trade and the Board of Agriculture on the Transatlantic Cattle Trade
Report (1890–91), LXXVIII, 269.
Departmental Committee appointed by the Board of Agriculture and Fisheries to enquire into and report upon the Fruit Industry of Great Britain (FI)
Reports: (1905), XX, 541; (1906), XXIV, 1.
Board of Agriculture and Fisheries: Report on the Decline in the Agricultural Population of Great Britain 1881–1906 (DAP)
Report (1906), XCVI, 586 (by R. H. Rew).
Private Ensilage Commission
Report (1884–5), XX, 179; (1886), XIX, 345.
Return of replies to questions . . . to persons who have silos etc (1884–5), LXXXIV, 295.

A number of important annual reports appear in *BPP*, notably:
Annual Report of the Veterinary Department (from 1871 under various titles; see p 190 of official index under 5). Contagious Diseases, Inspection and Transit of Animals, Weighing of Cattle etc, and p 191, 15 (Veterinary Department).
Agricultural Statistics (returns of crops and livestock from 1866, under various titles, see pp 22–3 of official index, also *A Century of Agricultural Statistics* below).
Reports on Woods, Forests and Land Revenues of Crown (see p 1530 of official index).

The many other *BPP* items are best located through either the official index or P. and G. Ford, *Select List of British Parliamentary Papers 1833–1899* (Oxford, 1953), of which the introduction is a useful general guide pointing out shortcomings in the official index.

Newspapers
Every newspaper of the period says—or sells—something of

the depression. Provincial weeklies are most useful despite political bias and uncertain areas of circulation. Those listed below have been used by the author. Material cited elsewhere in this bibliography often depends on other newspapers.

Bedfordshire Times and Independent, Bedford.
Chester Chronicle, Chester.
Dorset County Chronicle, Dorchester.
Peterborough Advertiser, Peterborough.
Westmoreland Gazette and Kendal Advertiser, Kendal.

Farming Journals

The selection of items below is drawn primarily from the annual volumes of the great agricultural societies: the *Journal of the Royal Agricultural Society of England (JRASE)* and the *Transactions of the Highland and Agricultural Society (HAS)*. It is no more than a selection. I have been unable to consult weekly farming newspapers such as the *Livestock Journal* and *Mark Lane Express.*

Allnutt, H. 'Diagrams showing the fluctuations in the recorded weekly average prices of wheat from 1863 to 1882 inclusive', *JRASE (series 2)*, 19 (1883), 206–8. The diagrams are on a weekly basis
Bear, W. E. 'Agricultural depression at home and abroad', *JRASE (series 3)*, 7 (1894), 673–95
Bear, W. E. 'The survival in farming', *JRASE (series 3)*, 2 (1891), 257–75
Cadle, C. E. 'Farming customs and covenants of England', *JRASE (series 2)*, 4 (1868), 144–75. Gives details of dates of entry, etc
Caird, J. B. 'Fifty years' progress of British agriculture', *JRASE (series 3)*, 1 (1890), 20–37
Caird, J. B. 'General view of British agriculture', *JRASE (series 2)*, 14 (1878), 273–332
Carrington, W. T. 'The advantage of converting cold day arable land into permanent pasture and the best method of doing it', *JRASE (series 2)*, 15 (1879), 487–97. An apt year to discuss the subject; papers on this topic are numerous
Druce, S. B. L. 'The alteration in the distribution of the agricultural population of England and Wales between the

census of 1871 and 1881', *JRASE (series 2)*, 21 (1885), 96–126

Dun, F. 'Report on Liver Rot', *JRASE (series 2)*, 17 (1881), 141–204

Elwes, H. J. and Malden, W. J. 'Cross-bred sheep', *JRASE (series 3)*, 6 (1895), 221–42

Evans, M. and Bowstead, T. 'Laying down land to permanent pasture', *JRASE (series 2)*, 11 (1875), 442–509

Fream, W. 'The decline of wheat-growing in England', *JRASE (series 2)*, 16 (1880), 435–41

Hutcheson, A. 'The past and future of Scottish agriculture', *HAS (series 5)*, 11 (1899), 121–35

Lawes, J. B. and Gilbert, J. H. 'On the home produce, imports, consumption, and price of wheat over twenty-eight (or twenty-seven) harvest years 1852–3 to 1879–80', *JRASE (series 2)*, 16 (1880), 337–54

McConnell, P. 'Experiences of a Scotsman on the Essex clays', *JRASE (series 3)*, 2 (1891), 311–25

MacDonald, A. 'The agriculture of the counties of Elgin and Nairn', *HAS (series 4)*, 16 (1884), 1–123

MacDonald, A. 'The agriculture of the county of Selkirk', *HAS (series 4)*, 18 (1886), 69–124. *JRASE* county essays are generally pre-depression

MacDonald, J. 'On the agriculture of the County of Sutherland', *HAS (series 4)*, 12 (1880), 1–90

Malden, W. J. 'Recent changes in farm practices', *JRASE (series 2)*, 22 (1886), 377–442

Morgan-Richardson, C. 'The story of a grass farm on clay', *Journal of the Bath and West and Southern Counties Soc (series 4)*, 10 (1899–1900), 34–43

Morton, J. C. 'The past agricultural year', *JRASE (series 2)*, 16 (1880), 210–49. The best contemporary view of 1879

Ralston, W. H. 'The agriculture of Wigtownshire', *HAS (series 4)*, 1 (1885), 92–133

Randell, C. 'Laying down clay-land intended for permanent pasture', *JRASE (series 2)*, 18 (1882), 368–70

Read, C. S. 'Large and small holdings: a comparative view', *JRASE (series 2)*, 23 (1887), 1–27

Rew, R. H. 'The agricultural situation in the west of England',

Journal of the Bath and West and Southern Counties Soc (series 4), 5 (1894–5), 62–78

Scott, J. 'British farming and foreign competition', *HAS (series 5)*, 5 (1893), 112–29

Sheldon, J. P. 'Report on the American and Canadian meat trade', *JRASE (series 2)*, 13 (1877), 295–355

Smyth, J. B. 'On the comparative return from capital invested in cropping, grazing, or planting land upon hill and moorland', *HAS (series 4)*, 10 (1878), 255–75

Speir, J. 'Change in cropping to suit altered conditions of farming', *HAS (series 5)*, 2 (1890), 65–78

Symons, G. J. 'Recent British weather', *JRASE (series 2)*, 19 (1883), 411–21

Wilson, J. 'Half a century as a Border farmer', *HAS (series 5)*, 15 (1902), 35–48

Wrightson, J. 'The agricultural lessons of "the eighties" ', *JRASE (series 3)*, 1 (1890), 275–88

Non-farming Journals
That the depression had no wide contemporary impact outside the world of farming is evidenced by the neglect of the topic in journals other than those devoted to economics and statistics:

Anon, 'The economic effects of cattle disease legislation', *EJ*, 15 (1905), 156–63

Anon, 'Scottish farming in Essex', *Country Life*, 8 (1900), 396–8

Bear, W. J. 'The agricultural problem', *EJ*, 3 (1893), 391–407

Bear, W. J. 'Our agricultural population', *EJ*, 4 (1894), 317–31

Fiamingo, G. M. 'The Agricultural Crisis,' *EJ*, 8 (1898), 259–64. On Italy. Continental prosperity generally attracted more notice than problems

Hardy, Thos. 'The Dorsetshire Labourer', *Longmans Magazine*, 2 (July 1883), 252–69

King, B. and Arch, J. 'Statistics of some Midland villages', *EJ*, 3 (1893), 1–22 and 193–204

Malden, W. J. 'The Greater Agriculture', *Nineteenth Century and After*, 437 (July 1913), 92–108

Price, L. L. 'The Commission on Agriculture', *EJ*, 6 (1896), 389–407

Price, L. L. 'The accounts of the Oxford colleges 1893–1903

with special reference to their agricultural revenues', 67 (1904), 585–660

Price, L. L. 'The recent depression in agriculture as shown in the accounts of an Oxford college 1876–90', *JRSS*, 55 (1892), 2–36

Roxby, P. M. 'Rural depopulation in England during the nineteenth century', *Nineteenth Century and After*, 431 (Jan 1912), 174–90

Steele, J. C. 'The agricultural depression and its effects on a leading London hospital', *JRSS*, 55 (1892), 37–48

Thompson, R. J. 'An enquiry into the rent of agricultural land in England and Wales in the nineteenth century', *JRSS*, 70 (1907), 587–616

Welton, T. A. 'On the distribution of population in England and Wales and its progress . . . 1890–91', *JRSS*, 63 (1900), 527–95

Farming Manuals

Elliot, R. H. *The agricultural changes required by these times and laying down land to grass,* 3rd ed (Kelso, 1905)

Long, J. *A Handbook for Farmers and Smallholders* (1892)

Prout, J. *Profitable Clay Farming* (1881)

Walker, J. *Farming to profit in modern times* (1888)

Wrightson, J. *Farm Crops* (1892)

Youatt, W. (ed Fream, W.) *The Complete Grazier* etc, 13th ed (1893)

Literature of the Period

Bedford, Duke of. *The Story of a Great Agricultural Estate (being the story of the origin and administration of Woburn and Thorney)* (1897)

Brodrick, G. C. *English Land and English Landlords* (1881)

Caird, J. B. *The Landed Interest and the Supply of Food* (1878, 5th ed with introduction by G. E. Mingay, 1967)

Channing, F. A. *The Truth about the Agricultural Depression* (1897)

Dunster, H. *How to make the land pay* (1885)

Gladstone, W. E. *Midlothian Speeches* (Victorian Library, Leicester, 1971)

Graham, P. A. *The Revival of English agriculture* (1899)

Graham, P. A. *The Rural Exodus: the problem of the village and the town* (1892)

Haggard, H. Rider. *Rural England* (1902)

Hall, A. D. *A Pilgrimage of British Farming* (1913)

Jefferies, R. *Hodge and His Masters* (1880). This is generally agreed to be his rustic masterpiece, a collection of newspaper pieces. Most of his other books of essays contain material on the depression. See also Perry, P. J., p 198

Jessopp, A. *Arcady for better for worse* (1887)

Pratt, E. A. *The Transition in Agriculture* (1906)

Rowntree, B. S. and Kendall, M. *How the Labourer Lives* (1913)

Tennyson, Lord, *Prefatory poem to my brother's sonnets: midnight, June 30th 1879*

Vincent, J. E. *The Land Question in North Wales: a brief survey of agrarian agitation* (1896). A conservative, pro-landlord critique of *WLC*

Wantage, Lady, *Lord Wantage, VC, KCB. A memoir by his wife* (1907)

Unpublished Primary Sources
This book depends on the great variety of material of this kind used by both contemporary commentators and three generations of scholars; newspapers provide an exact parallel. My own use of such materials has been limited to no more than a few days in the Dorset and Bedfordshire Record Offices and in the Digby Estate Office, Sherborne. Such materials as rent accounts, estate memoranda, valuations, diaries, family papers, have therefore played a small part directly but a very great part indirectly in the writing of this book. Such material is referred to specifically in the notes in the few appropriate cases.

Farming Reminiscences
The less known items are often more useful than the classics:

'Bourne, G.' (pseudonym of Sturt, G.) *Change in Our Village* (1911). Surrey

Bradley, A. G. *When Squires and Farmers Thrived* (1927). Lothians

Cornish, J. G. *Reminiscences of Country Life* (1939). Berkshire

Gibb, R. S. *A Farmer's Fifty Years in Lauderdale* (1927). Borders

Hudson, W. *A Shepherd's Life* (1910). Wiltshire

Keith, J. *Fifty Years of Farming* (1953). Aberdeenshire

Kendall, S. G. *Farming Memoirs of a West Country Yeoman* (1944). Somerset and Wiltshire

Savory, A. H. *Grain and Chaff from an English Manor* (1920). Worcestershire

Smith, D. *No Rain in these Clouds* (1943). Essex

Street, A. G. *Farmer's Glory* (1932). Wiltshire

Street, A. G. *The Gentleman of the Party* (1936). Wiltshire

Thompson, F. *Lark Rise to Candleford* (1939 et seq). Northants

Secondary Sources

Ashby, M. K. *Joseph Ashby of Tysoe* (Cambridge 1961)

Ashworth, W. *An economic history of England 1870–1939* (1960)

Astor, W. (Viscount) and Rowntree, B. Seebohm. *British Agriculture: the principles of future policy* (1939). Chapter 3 (63–98) discusses the changing structure of British agriculture 1868–1938

Bainbridge, T. 'Some factors in the development of Cumbrian agriculture especially during the nineteenth century', *Trans of the Cumberland and Westmorland Arch and Antiq Soc*, 44 (1945), 81–93

Beales, H. E. ' "The Great Depression" in industry and trade', *EcHR*, 5 no 1 (1934), 65–75

Beastall, T. W. 'A south Yorkshire estate in the late nineteenth century', *AgHR*, 14 no 1 (1966), 40–44

Beavington, F. 'Early market gardening in Bedfordshire', *IBG*, 37 (December 1965), 91–100

Bellerby, J. R. and Boreham, A. J. 'Farm occupiers' capital in the United Kingdom before 1939', *Farm Economist*, 7 no 6 (1952–4), 257–63

Besse, P. *La crise et l'évolution de l'agriculture en Angleterre de 1875 à nos jours* (Paris, 1910)

Britton, D. K. and Rhée, H. A. *The rent of agricultural land in England and Wales 1870–1946* (for the Country

Landowners' Association, the Ministry of Agriculture, Fisheries and Food, and the Oxford University Institute of Agricultural Economics, 1949)

Burnet, John. *Plenty and Want: a social history of diet in England from 1815 to the present day* (1966).

A Century of Agricultural Statistics: Great Britain 1866–1966 (HMSO 1968)

Chadwick, W. Owen. *The Victorian Church, Part 2 1860–1901* (1970)

Checkland, S. G. *The rise of industrial society in England 1815–85* (1964)

Clapham, Sir John, *An Economic History of Modern Britain:* Volume 2, *Free Trade and Steel 1850–86* (Cambridge, 1932) and Volume 3, *Machines and National Rivalries 1887–1914* (Cambridge, 1936)

Clark, G. S. R. Kitson, *The making of Victorian England* (1962)

Collins, E. J. T. and Jones, E. L. 'Sectoral advances in English agriculture 1850–1880', *AgHR,* 15 no 2 (1967), 65–81. Replying to Sturgess, R. W.

Conacher, H. M. 'Causes of the fall in agricultural prices between 1875 and 1895', *Scottish Journal of Agriculture,* 19 (1936), 219–24

Coppock, J. T. 'Agricultural changes in the Chilterns 1875–1900', *AgHR,* 9 no 1 (1961), 1–16

Coppock, J. T. 'The agricultural returns as a source for local history', *Amateur Historian,* 4 no 2 (1958–9), 49–55

Coppock, J. T. 'The changing arable in the Chilterns 1875–1951', *Geography,* 42 no 4 (1957), 217–29

Coppock, J. T. 'The changing arable in England and Wales 1870–1956', *Tidschrift voor Economische en Sociale Geografie,* 50 no 6/7 (1959), 121–30

Coppock, J. T. 'The statistical assessment of British agriculture', *AgHR,* 4 no 1 (1956), 4–21 and 4 no 2 (1956), 66–79

Coulton, G. G. *Fourscore years: an autobiography* (Cambridge, 1943)

Critchell, J. T. and Raymond, J. *A History of the Frozen Meat Trade* (1912)

Darby, H. C. 'The draining of the English claylands', *Geographische Zeitschrift,* 52 no 3 (1964), 190–201

N

Darby, H. C. 'The Lincolnshire Wolds', *Lincolnshire Historian,* 9 (1952), 315–324

Denman, D. R. *Tenant-right valuation; in history and modern practice* (Cambridge, 1942)

Dovring, F. 'The transformation of European agriculture', in Habakkuk, H. J. and Postan, M. (eds), *Cambridge Economic History of Europe* (Cambridge, 1966), Volume 6, Pt 2, Chapter 6, 604–72

Drescher, L. 'The development of agricultural production in Great Britain and Ireland from the early nineteenth century', *Manchester School,* 33 no 2 (1955), 153–83. With comment by T. W. Fletcher. The article is translated from the German of 1935

Dulac, A. *L'agriculture et le libre-échange dans le Royaume Uni* (Paris, 1903)

Dunbabin, J. P. D. 'The incidence and organisation of agricultural trades unionism in the 1870s', *AgHR,* 16 no 2 (1968), 114–41

Eagle, E. C. 'Some light on the beginnings of the Lincolnshire bulb industry', *Lincolnshire Historian,* 6 (1950), 220–9

Emery, F. E. and Oeser, O. A. *Information, decision and action: a study of psychological determinants of changes in farming techniques* (Melbourne, 1958)

Ernle, Lord. See Prothero, R. E.

Evans, G. E. *The Horse in the Furrow* (1960)

Evans, G. E. *Where beards wag all—the relevance of the oral tradition* (1970)

Fairlie, S. 'The Corn Laws and British wheat production 1829–76', *EcHR (series 2),* 22 no 1 (1969), 88–116

Firey, W. *Man, mind and land: a theory of resource use* (Glencoe, Illinois 1960)

Flavigny, P. *Le régime agraire en Angleterre au dixneuvième siècle et la concentration d'exploitation* (Paris 1932)

Fletcher, T. W. 'The great depression of English agriculture 1873–96', *EcHR (series 2),* 13 no 3 (1960–61), 417–32

Fletcher, T. W. 'Lancashire Livestock farming during the great depression', *AgHR,* 9 no 1 (1961), 17–42

Franklin, T. B. *British grasslands from the earliest times to the present day* (1953)

Fraser, P. *Joseph Chamberlain* (1966)

Fussell, G. W. 'Cornish farming 1500–1910', *Amateur Historian*, 4 no 8 (1960), 338–45

Fussell, G. E. *The English Dairy Farmer 1500–1900* (1966)

Fussell, G. E. 'Four centuries of Cheshire farming', *Trans of the Hist Soc of Lancashire and Cheshire*, 106 (1954), 57–79

Fussell, G. E. 'Four centuries of farming systems in Derbyshire: 1500–1900', *Journal of the Derbyshire Arch and Nat Hist Soc*, 71 (new series 24) (1951), 1–37

Fussell, G. E. 'Four centuries of farming systems in Dorset', *Proc of Dorset Nat Hist and Arch Soc*, 73 (1952), 116–41

Fussell, G. E. 'Four centuries of farming systems in Shropshire', *Trans of the Shropshire Archaeological Society*, 54 (1953), 1–29

Fussell, G. E. 'Four centuries of farming systems in Sussex, 1500–1900', *Sussex Archaeological Collections*, 90 (1952), 60–102

Fussell, G. E. 'Four centuries of Leicestershire farming', in Hoskins, W. G. *Studies in Leicestershire Agricultural History*, (Leicester 1949), 154–76

Fussell, G. E. 'Four centuries of Lincolnshire farming', *Reports and papers—Lincolnshire Architectural and Archaeological Soc*, 4 no 2 (1952), 109–30

Fussell, G. E. 'Glamorgan farming: an outline of its modern history', *Morgannwg*, 1 (1957), 31–43

Fussell, G. E. 'The grasses and grassland cultivation of Britain: II, 1700–1900', *Journal of the British Grassland Soc*, 19 no 2 (1964), 212–17

Fussell, G. E. 'Potatoes to the rescue in 1894', *Suffolk Review*, 1 (1956), 8–10

Fussell, G. E. 'Welsh farming in 1879', *Trans of the Hon Soc of Cymmrodorion* (1938), 247–55

Garnett, F. W. *Westmorland agriculture, 1800–1900* (Kendal, 1912)

Gavin, Sir Wm. *Ninety years of family farming: the story of Lord Rayleigh's and Strutt and Parker farms* (1967)

Grant, I. F. 'Three official reports upon the agricultural depression', *Economica*, No 12 (November 1924), 336–52. A misleading title in this context; it is concerned primarily with postwar depression, but some comparisons are made with the situation in the 1880s

Green, F. E. *A history of the English agricultural labourer 1870–1920* (1920)

Grigg, D. B. 'The development of tenant-right in south Lincolnshire', *Lincolnshire Historian*, 2 no 9 (1962), 41–47

Halèvy, E. *A history of the English people in the nineteenth century: V. Imperialism and the rise of labour*, 2nd ed (1951)

Hammond, J. *Livestock changes in Norfolk since the year 1780* (Sprowston, Norfolk, 1957)

Harvey, N. 'A clayland farmer in the bad times', *Journal of the Chartered Land Agents Society*, 69 (February 1960)

Harvey, N. *A History of Farm Buildings in England and Wales* (1970)

Havinden, M. et al, *Estate villages* (1967). An account of the development of Lord Wantage's estates

Hertfordshire, Bedfordshire and Buckinghamshire Agricultural Valuers' Association Centennial Volume (1950)

Hunt, E. H. 'Labour productivity in British agriculture 1850–1914', *EcHR (series 2)*, 20 no 2 (1967), 280–92: also rejoinder 22 no 1 (1969), 118–19. See also Metcalf, D.

Jones, E. G. 'The Argentine refrigerated meat industry', *Economica*, no 26 (June 1929), 156–73

Jones, E. L. 'The changing basis of English agricultural prosperity 1853–73', *AgHR*, 10 no 2 (1963), 102–19

Jones, E. L. 'English farming before and during the nineteenth century', *EcHR (series 2)*, 15 no 1 (1962), 145–52. Reviewing a new edition of Ernle

Jones, E. L. 'Land utilisation changes and weather conditions on the Marlborough Downs c 1500–1960: the possibility of catastrophe to the *Cepaea Nemoralis* population', *Phil Trans of the Royal Soc of London (series B)*, 246 (1963), 30–31

Jones, E. L. *Seasons and prices: the role of the weather in English agricultural history* (1964)

Jones, G. P. and Pool, A. G. *A hundred years of economic development in Great Britain* (1940)

Kerr, B. *Bound to the Soil* (1968). Dorset

Layton, Sir W. T. and Crowther, G. *The Study of Prices* (1935)

Lloyd, T. *The General Election of 1880* (Oxford, 1968)

Londonderry, Marchioness of. *Henry Chaplin—A Memoir* (1926)

McDowell, R. B. *British Conservatism 1832–1914* (1959)

MacGregor, J. J. 'Recent land-tenure changes in mid-Devon', *Economica (new series)*, 1 no 4 (1934), 459–72

MacGregor, J. J. *History of landownership since 1870 with special reference to conditions in Cambridgeshire* (unpublished thesis for BLitt, Oxford University 1938)

Martin, E. W. *The secret people* (1954)

Martin, E. W. *The shearers and the shorn—a study of Life in a Devon community* (1965)

Matthews, A. H. H. *Fifty years of agricultural politics 1865–1915* (1915). A jubilee history of the Central Chamber of Agriculture

Maxton, J. P. *Landownership in Scotland in its relation to the economic development of agriculture in the period 1871–1921* (unpublished thesis for BLitt, Oxford University 1930)

May, A. E. 'What Essex farms cost forty years ago', *Essex Review*, 254 (April 1955), 83–5

Metcalf, D. 'A theoretical comment', *EcHR (series 2)*, 22 no 1 (1965), 117–18. Replying to Hunt, E. H.

Murray, K. A. H. *Factors affecting the price of livestock in Great Britain: a preliminary study* (Oxford, 1931)

Musson, A. E. 'The great depression in Britain 1873–96: a reappraisal', *Journal of Economic History*, 19 no 2 (1959), 199–228

Ojala, E. M. *Agriculture and economic progress* (1952)

Olson, M. and Harris, C. C. 'Free trade in "corn": a statistical study of the prices and production of wheat in Great Britain from 1873 to 1914', *Quarterly Journal of Economics*, 73 no 1 (1959), 145–168

Orr, J. *Agriculture in Oxfordshire* (Oxford, 1916)

Orr, J. *Agriculture in Berkshire* (Oxford, 1918)

Orwin, C. S. and Whetham, E. H. *History of British Agriculture, 1846–1914* (1964)

Parker, J. Oxley (ed). *The Oxley Parker papers* (Colchester, 1964)

Partridge, M. *Early agricultural machinery* (1969)

Perren, R. 'The landlord and agricultural transformation 1870–1900', *AgHR*, 18 no 1 (1970), 36–51

Perren, R. 'The North American beef and cattle trade with

Great Britain, 1870–1914', *EcHR (series 2)*, 24 no 3 (1971), 430–44

Perry, P. J. 'An agricultural journalist on the "great depression": Richard Jefferies', *Journal of British Studies*, 9 no 2 (1970), 126–40

Perry, P. J. 'A source for agricultural history: newspaper advertisements', *The Local Historian*, 9 no 7 (1971), 334–7

Perry, P. J. (ed), *British Agriculture 1870–1914* (Debates in Economic History, 1973)

Perry, P. J. 'Where was the "great agricultural depression": a geography of agricultural bankruptcy in late Victorian England and Wales', *AgHR*, 20 (1972), 30–45

Perry, P. J. and Johnston, R. J. 'The temporal and spatial incidence of agricultural depression in Dorset, 1868–1902', *Journal of Interdisciplinary History*, 3 no 2 (1972), 297–311

Phelps-Brown, E. J. and Handfield-Jones, S. J. 'The climacteric of the 1890s: a study in the expanding economy', *Oxford Economic Papers (new series)*, 4 no 3 (1952), 266–307

Phillips, A. D. M. 'Underdraining and the English claylands 1850–1880: a review', *AgHR*, 17 no 1 (1969), 44–55

Pickerill, N. L. *Straight Furrows* (1950)

Prothero, R. E. (Lord Ernle). *English Farming Past and Present* (1912). Reprinted in 1961 with introduction by G. E. Fussell and O. R. McGregor

Reeve, F. A. *Cambridge* (1964)

Rew, R. H. *An agricultural faggot* (1913). A collection of papers by one of the 'experts' among late Victorian agricultural writers; none of the others appear to have produced a similar volume

Rosenberg, H. 'Political and social consequences of the great depression of 1873–96', *EcHR,* 13 no 1 and 2 (1943), 58–73

Rowe, J. 'Cornish agriculture in the age of the great depression, 1875–1895', *Journal of the Royal Institution of Cornwall (new series)*, 3 (1957–60), 147–62

Ruston, A. G. and Witney, D. *Hooton Pagnell: the agricultural evolution of a Yorkshire village* (1934)

Saul, S. B. *The myth of the great depression* (1969)

Sayers, R. S. *A history of economic change in England, 1880–1939* (1967)

Scott, J. W. Robertson. *England's green and pleasant-land* (1925)

Skeel, C. 'The cattle trade between England and Wales from the fifteenth century to the nineteenth century', *Trans of the Royal Hist Soc (series 4)*, 9 (1926), 135–58

Smith, E. Lorrain, *Go east for a farm: a study of rural migration* (Oxford, 1932)

Smith, J. H. 'The cattle trade of Aberdeenshire in the nineteenth century', *AgHR*, 3 no 2 (1955), 114–18

Smith, M. W. 'Snape—a modern example of depopulation', *Wiltshire Arch and Nat Hist Magazine*, 57 (1958–60), 386–90

Spence, C. C. *God Speed the plow: the coming of steam cultivation to Britain* (Urbana, Illinois, 1960)

Spring, D. *The English landed estate in the nineteenth century: its administration* (Baltimore, 1963)

Stapledon, R. G. and Davies, W. *Ley farming* (1941)

Stevens, P. G. *Sheep: part 2, sheep farming development and sheep breeds in New Zealand* (Christchurch, 1961). Valuable on the early history of the frozen lamb trade

Sturgess, R. W. 'The agricultural revolution on the English clays', *AgHR*, 14 no 2 (1966), 104–121; also a rejoinder, *AgHR*, 15 no 2 (1967), 82–7. See also Collins, E. J. T. and Jones, E. L.

Sutherland, D. *The Landowners* (1968)

Symon, J. A. 'Cairnhill, Turriff 1861–1926', *Scottish Agriculture* 30 and 31 (1951), 199–202 and 24–9

Symon, J. A. *Scottish farming past and present* (Edinburgh, 1959)

Taylor, A. M. *Gillett's: Bankers at Banbury and Oxford* (Oxford, 1964)

Tavener, L. E. 'Whither sheep. A review of the decline of sheep farming in Dorset', *Notes and Queries for Somerset and Dorset*, 26 no 134 (1955), 173–6

Thirsk, J. *English peasant farming: the agrarian history of Lincolnshire from Tudor to recent times* (1957)

Thirsk, J. and Imray, J. 'Suffolk farming in the nineteenth century', *Suffolk Record Soc,* 1 (1958)

Thompson, F. M. L. 'Agricultural History', *History*, 48 (1963), 28–33

Thompson, F. M. L. 'English great estates in the nineteenth century, 1790–1914', *Proc of the first int conf of econ hist* (Stockholm, 1960), 385–97

Thompson, F. M. L. *English landed society in the nineteenth century* (1963)

Thompson, F. M. L. 'Land and politics in England in the nineteenth century', *Trans of the Royal Hist Soc (series 5)*, 15 (1965), 23–44

Thompson, F. M. L. 'The land market in the nineteenth century', *Oxford Economic Papers (new series)*, 9 no 3 (1957), 285–308

Thompson, F. M. L. 'The second agricultural revolution 1815–1880', *EcHR (series 2)*, 21 no 1 (1968), 62–77

Trow-Smith, R. *A history of British livestock husbandry 1700–1900* (1959)

Trow-Smith, R. *Society and the land* (1952)

Venn, J. A. *The foundations of agricultural economics* (Cambridge, 1923)

Victoria County History of England. The following are useful: Anderson, R. 'Gloucestershire' (Vol 2, 1907), 239–62; Biddell, H. 'Suffolk' (Vol 2, 1907), 385–402; Buckle, A. J. H. 'Dorset' (Vol 2, 1908), 278–86; Collins, G. E. 'Lincolnshire' (Vol 2, 1906), 397–416; Crittall, E. 'Wiltshire' (Vol 4, 1959), 369–77; Curtler, W. R. H. 'Herefordshire' (Vol 1, 1908) 407–28; Curtler, W. R. H. 'Lancashire' (Vol 2, 1908), 419–36; Ditchfield, P. H. and Simmons, W. A. 'Berkshire' (Vol 2, 1907), 331–41; Ingram, W. F. 'Sussex' (Vol 2, 1907), 273–90; Newton, J. 'Yorkshire' (Vol 2, 1910), 455–80; Spencer, A. J. 'Surrey' (Vol 4, 1912), 455–64; Thirsk, J. 'Leicestershire' (Vol 2, 1954), 199–253; Thompson, F. M. L. 'Wiltshire' (Vol 4, 1959), 92–114; Walker, E. G. F. 'Somerset' (Vol 2, 1911), 533–46

Ward, J. C. 'The Beaumont family's estate in the nineteenth century', *Bull of the Inst of Hist Research*, 35 (1962), 168–77

Ward, J. T. *East Yorkshire landed estates in the nineteenth century* (York, 1967, as no 23 of E. Yorkshire local history series)

Ward, J. T. 'Farm sale prices over a hundred years', *Estates Gazette (centennial supplement)*, 171 (May 1958), 47–9

Watson, J. A. Scott. *The History of the Royal Agricultural Society of England 1839–1939* (1939)

Whetham, E. H. 'The changing cattle enterprise of England

and Wales 1870–1910', *Geographical Journal,* 129 no 3 (1963), 378–80

Whetham, E. H. 'Livestock prices in Britain 1851–93', *AgHR,* 11 no 1 (1963), 27–35

Whetham, E. H. 'The London milk trade 1860–1900', *EcHR (series 2),* 17 no 2 (1964–5), 369–80

Wilson, C. H. 'Economy and society in late Victorian Britain', *EcHR (series 2),* 18 no 1 (1965), 183–98

Wingfield-Stratford, E. *The squire and his relations* (1956)

Wolpert, J. 'The decision process in a spatial context', *Annals of the Association of American Geographers,* 54 no 4 (1964) 537–58

Index